Autism and Buddhist Practice

of related interest

Asperger's Syndrome and Mindfulness
Taking Refuge in Buddha
Chris Mitchell
ISBN 978 1 84310 686 9
eISBN 978 1 84642 888 3

Mindful Living with Asperger's Syndrome
Everyday Mindfulness Practices to Help You Tune in to the Present Moment
Chris Mitchell
ISBN 978 1 84905 434 8
eISBN 978 0 85700 867 1

Autism and Spirituality
Psyche, Self and Spirit in People on the Autism Spectrum
Olga Bogdashina
ISBN 978 1 84905 285 6
eISBN 978 0 85700 591 5

Spirituality and the Autism Spectrum
Of Falling Sparrows
Abe Isanon
ISBN 978 1 84310 026 3
eISBN 978 0 85700 178 8

From Hurt to Hope
Stories of Mental Health, Mental Illness and Being Autistic
Edited by Mair Elliot
ISBN 978 1 78775 585 7
eISBN 978 1 78775 586 4

The Guide to Good Mental Health on the Autism Spectrum
Yenn Purkis, Emma Goodall and Jane Nugent
Forewords by Wenn Lawson and Kirsty Dempster-Rivett
ISBN 978 1 84905 670 0
eISBN 978 1 78450 195 2

Autism and Buddhist Practice

*How Buddhism Can Help Autistic
Adults Cultivate Wellbeing*

EDITED BY CHRIS JARRELL

Jessica Kingsley Publishers
London and Philadelphia

First published in Great Britain in 2023 by Jessica Kingsley Publishers
An imprint of Hodder & Stoughton Ltd
An Hachette UK Company

3

Copyright © Jessica Kingsley Publishers 2023

Front cover image source: Chris Jarrell.

A CIP catalogue record for this title is available from the
British Library and the Library of Congress

ISBN 978 1 83997 157 0
eISBN 978 1 83997 158 7

Printed and bound by CPI Group (UK) Ltd, Croydon, CR0 4YY

Jessica Kingsley Publishers' policy is to use papers that are natural,
renewable and recyclable products and made from wood grown in
sustainable forests. The logging and manufacturing processes are expected
to conform to the environmental regulations of the country of origin.

Jessica Kingsley Publishers
Carmelite House
50 Victoria Embankment
London EC4Y 0DZ

www.jkp.com

'Negative thoughts can often cloud the minds of autistic individuals. This is due to the fact that life has been extremely challenging. It's important that when these thoughts occur you do not let them take over and pull you down. Finding ways to accept, channel, and manage this is very helpful.'

Sarah Heath (2016, p155)

'In essence, the Buddha's teaching on the Four Noble Truths leads us first to a profound recognition of the origins of suffering; then to the recognition of the origins of suffering; then to a recognition of the possibility of the cessation of suffering; and, finally, to a recognition of the path that leads to such freedom.'

The Dalai Lama (2004, p13)

Contents

Acknowledgements

I would like to acknowledge the help of the following people in the compilation of this anthology. First of all, Lynda Cooper from Jessica Kingsley Publishers for spotting the potential of my book proposal and working with me and the contributors to bring the manuscript through to the production stage. The Rev. Sumi Loundon Kim at Yale for her invaluable practical advice and moral support in the planning and implementation of the project. Thanks also to Sister Linh Di and Mark Cooper for their valuable insights into the section 'What the Buddha Taught' in this book's introduction. The many Dharma teachers, Dharma centre directors and administrators, practice group coordinators and group leaders that forwarded my call for submissions through emails, newsletters, online posts and by word of mouth. All of the autistic people who contacted me to give me encouragement as well as to challenge my use of language and correct my understanding of the Dharma, and who also passed the call for submissions on to friends and colleagues. Thank you to Barry Taylor, for his input on Theravada Buddhism in 'What the Buddha Taught', and Sian Atkins, for her critical reading of the section 'Understanding Autism', also in the introduction. And, of course, all of the contributors to the anthology, both autistic and neurotypical, who gave their

time and energy in working collaboratively with me. Thank you
for trusting me with your stories.

And finally, the worlds of both Buddhism and autism can
be both culturally and politically complex. I have attempted
to take a middle way through this landscape while compiling
this anthology. However, I acknowledge responsibility for any
factual inaccuracies or biases you may come across despite my
efforts. And I apologize in advance for any cultural insensitiv-
ities that you, either as an autistic person, a Buddhist practitioner or both, may be offended by whilst reading this book.
I hope that this does not detract from you finding the book a
useful insight into the lives of the autistic Buddhists that are
illustrated herein.

Editor's Preface

I first came to Buddhism in the early 1990s when I attended an Order of Interbeing retreat in Scotland led by Sister Annabel Laity. It was then that I learned about mindfulness and its application to everyday life. I had always been an anxious personality, a loner and felt very different to other people. The silence of the retreat, the routine of each day and the lack of informal small talk suited me well. Mindfulness began to help me manage my anxiety, which was increasingly associated with social interactions and relationships, both at home and at work.

It was not until 30 years later that I was diagnosed with autism, at the age of 65, and I began to understand my life differently. In the interim I had deepened my understanding of the Buddha's teachings and associated practices such as meditation and mindfulness. The bringing together of this simple but profound philosophy on the nature of existence, and the logical and practical theory of mind, made sense to me. And now, it also sits well with my developing understanding of how autism has influenced me over the years, and still influences me today. My chosen spiritual path is helping me to integrate my understanding of autism into my life. It helps me to make sense of what often seems like a confusing and overwhelming social and emotional landscape. It also gives me practical ways of negotiating the stress and anxiety that is still a feature of my daily life, although less so now I am retired.

An increasing number of autistic people are finding Buddhist practices such as meditation and mindfulness helpful in improving mental health and wellbeing. This growing interest is reflected in books such as *Mindful Living with Asperger's Syndrome*[1] by Chris Mitchell and *The Autistic Buddha* by Tom Clements – both of whom are autistic. There are also various blogs and YouTube videos posted by autistic people who are actively embracing Buddhist teachings and practices, known as the Dharma. And it was when exploring these accounts online that the ideas behind this book began to arise.

Having been recently diagnosed as autistic, I wanted to meet other autistic people who had a similar approach to life as me. These books and online posts were, I suspected, just the tip of the iceberg. I was curious and decided to reach out to other autistic people who had taken refuge in the Buddha, the Dharma and the Sangha. I wanted to hear their stories – what helped and hindered their progress on their chosen spiritual path.

The starting point for networking to find the people I wanted to talk to was the large network of Buddhist centres, communities and meditation groups across the UK and the USA. I had a hunch that this was where the autistic people with whom I wanted to connect could be found. My hope was that they had stories to tell, and would be willing and able to write them down for inclusion in an anthology of personal stories.

Within a week of sending out the first networking email in the UK I received positive replies from autistic people as well as neurotypical people who either parented, advocated on

---

[1]   **Asperger's syndrome** is an older term for a form of autism that has now been subsumed into Autism Spectrum Disorder in the DSM-5.

behalf of or taught autistic people. It seemed like my hunch was bearing out. Soon I was in Zoom conversations with people, both neurodiverse and neurotypical, who had been practising Buddhists for many years. The writing process had begun and stories had started to arrive in my mailbox. It became apparent to me that I was not the only autistic person who had taken refuge in the logical philosophy of life that Buddhism offers. I was not alone in welcoming Buddhist Precepts, the Four Noble Truths and the Noble Eightfold Path, together with practices such as meditation and mindfulness, into my life. I had found my spiritual community, my sangha. It was also clear that Buddhism was a source of compassion and support for parents and teachers of autistic people, and it became increasingly apparent that their stories should also be included in this anthology.

Working with the writers in the compilation of this anthology soon became a privilege and a source of wonder as their often-moving stories unfolded on the page. My hope is that you too will be moved by their honesty and clarity and be inspired, if you are autistic, to follow their example, develop your understanding of Buddhism and then go on to deepen your practice. If you are a Dharma teacher, centre director or group leader, my hope is that these stories will both inform and motivate you to take some time out, either alone or with colleagues, to consider how you can develop your 'autism sensitive practice'.

Introduction

CHRIS JARRELL

If you are one of those autistic people who are increasingly using meditation and mindfulness techniques to manage your mental health and improve your wellbeing, this book is for you. I think that you will recognize many of the experiences that the contributors share about being autistic in a neurotypical world. You will empathize with their suffering and be inspired to follow their example. By exploring the basics of Buddhism presented in this book, and by developing your meditation and mindfulness practice further, you will be able to transform your suffering and increase your sense of wellbeing.

This book is also for Buddhist teachers, centre directors and meditation group leaders who want to find out more about developing 'autism sensitive practice' and how they can help autistic people in accessing Buddhist communities. You will find the ideas and suggestions integrated into the stories of us autistic Buddhists, and Appendix 1: A Short Guide to Autism Sensitive Practice, a useful addition to your discussions around increasing diversity in Buddhist communities.

Some autistic people find deepening their understanding of Buddhist teachings, known as the Dharma, or taking their Buddhist practice further, difficult. This is, perhaps, because they don't have a local meditation centre or group to attend and receive support from. Or it may be because, like me, they have difficulty attending groups for the first time, let alone going back a second time. (My experience of being autistic is that I am ambivalent about joining groups – I could quite happily be a hermit, but I also need human contact and companionship.)

The purpose of this book is to help autistic people like you and me make informed choices when considering whether to go further than the secular use of Buddhist practices such as meditation and mindfulness. It is possible to deepen your practice of meditation and mindfulness by joining a spiritual community, known in Buddhism as a sangha, and receive the encouragement and support of like-minded people. It is also possible to learn about the everyday application of Buddhist teachings, such as the Four Noble Truths and the Noble Eight-fold Path, by attending introductory courses, either in person or online.

The stories in this book also illustrate how autistic people have managed to deal with some of the problems they have experienced in accessing a spiritual community. These stories are about adversity, but they are also about hope and positive outcomes as the contributors tell how they have overcome their difficulties and have gone on to improve their wellbeing as a result. The writers who have contributed to this anthology also provide examples of what teachings and practices they have found useful, how they have adapted them to suit their own needs (often the need to not be overwhelmed by information and people) and how they have found creative ways of being part of a sangha.

If you are autistic and considering exploring Buddhism, the next section is intended to give you a simple overview of what can often be a complex and confusing area of study. This will help you put the stories in this anthology in context.

You will also find it useful to keep this information in mind when taking the next steps towards deepening your meditation and mindfulness practice with the help of a sangha.

WHAT THE BUDDHA TAUGHT

The starting point for any exploration of Buddhism, regardless of which school you adhere to, is that our suffering is real. Nothing amazing in that, you may think, but it's surprising how many of us spend so much time and energy avoiding suffering by attaching to people and things that we think will make us happy, or avoiding people and things that make us unhappy.

The Buddha came to this simple understanding as he meditated and reflected on how we live our lives. The first teaching the Buddha presented, over 2000 years ago, was on the Four Noble Truths and the Noble Eightfold Path.

- The First Noble Truth – simply that suffering (Dukkha) exists. In its everyday form, it is the suffering of, for example, birth, illness, injury and death. Psychologically, it is the suffering of attachment and aversion as our world is constantly changing around, and within, us and we attempt to stay in control. And spiritually, it is caused by being ignorant of the conditions that cause us to repeat our harmful thoughts, speech and actions – keeping us in a cycle of rebirth and suffering known in Buddhism as Samsara.

- The Second Noble Truth – the logical view that if suffering exists, it must have a cause, because of the law of cause and effect. Once we accept our suffering is real, we can turn towards its causes through meditation and other practices, rather than deny it.

- The Third Noble Truth – that given that there are causes to our suffering, by transforming these causes our suffering will cease to exist, and we will be happy. If we are able to transform the painful feelings and difficult thoughts that cloud our minds, we can experience happiness.

- The Fourth Noble Truth – that there is a path that leads us to happiness and wellbeing, known as the Noble Eightfold Path. This path provides us with an opportunity to transform our negative thoughts and difficult feelings, and find true community and wellbeing.

The Four Noble Truths and the Noble Eightfold Path are there at the beginning of any study of Buddhism, but are not always obvious when we pick up a book, listen to an online talk or attend a Buddhist centre or meditation event for the first time. The Noble Eightfold Path encompasses much of the Buddha's philosophy of the nature of reality; his theory of mind; the values and qualities we must develop in order to progress on the path to wellbeing; the practices of meditation and mindfulness; and an ethical framework that guides our thinking, speech, behaviour and choice of livelihoods.

It's worth reading up on the different contemporary approaches and schools of Buddhism that have developed from the two main traditions that have survived over the millennia – Theravada and Mahayana. Take some time to consider what you are looking for in terms of a spiritual path. Reflect on what kind of practice suits you best and which cultural representation of Buddhism suits your sensibilities. For example, the Theravada tradition, which is close to the original teachings of the Buddha, encourages meditation, reflection and insight. Whereas some approaches within the Mahayana tradition, such as Zen, are more focused on silence and meditation. Other schools, such as Vajrayana, employ prostrations, chanting and the visualization of deities such as Avalokiteshvara as a means of purifying the mind.

Just like when choosing a counsellor or a therapist, take some time to shop around, try out different workshops (either online or by attending an event) and get the feel of what suits you best. If you are able to, visit different groups and see what kind of welcome you get. As an autistic person I have never felt unwelcomed by a sangha, although it has always been difficult to walk through the door for the first time. My capacity to tolerate being in groups limits the time I can spend with a sangha – either on an event-by-event basis or over a longer period of time. As expectations grow that my relationships with sangha should deepen and become mutually supportive, I usually start to struggle.

It is for you as an individual to make your choices about which school of Buddhism you wish to follow, and how you consequently develop your understanding of the Buddha's core teachings. Theravada and Mahayana centres and meditation groups will guide you on your chosen path, provide you with educational opportunities and give you the chance to practise meditation and mindfulness according to their tradition. Like a number of the contributors to this anthology, you can always move from school to school, or centre to centre, until you feel at home. By the way, you should be mindful of getting caught up in Buddhist cults, which can be harmful. If the teachings are too dogmatic and actively exclude other ideas and approaches; if your participation in the community is dependent on a financial contribution; or if the community is led by a strong, charismatic personality that does not encourage debate and challenge, then alarm bells should be ringing. Many contemporary Buddhist organizations are developing safeguarding policies and, if you are worried or concerned, refer to these documents and discuss your worries with a trusted friend or professional.

The next section will be of help to you if you are a Buddhist teacher, centre manager or meditation group leader. It will help raise your awareness of autism and increase your understanding of why we autistic people think and behave in the way that we do. You may not be aware, at first, that you are speaking to an autistic person. Some of us may seem reserved and distant, others may be quite the opposite and engage in a very energetic and sometimes forthright way. Often, we will appear for one session and then not come back, as joining groups can be particularly challenging for us. Here are some of the reasons why.

UNDERSTANDING AUTISM

As an autistic man, I want to be part of society in a way that suits my individual sensitivities and abilities; allows me to participate in educational and work opportunities, relationships and family life; and provides me with opportunities to follow a spiritual path. Nothing surprising about that, you may think. We all want the same thing. But what may surprise you is that it is estimated that there are around 700,000 autistic people in the UK (The National Autistic Society, 2022), roughly 3.5 million autistic people in the USA (Autism Society, 2020), and about 350,000 autistic people in Australia (Autism Spectrum Australia, 2018).

We are all, it's reasonable to assume, just the same as everybody else in that we want to live our lives as fully and as happily as possible. But most autistic people experience significant difficulties, to varying degrees, with social communication and interaction in a way that impedes our daily lives and relationships. The world can often seem a confusing and bewildering place to be in and we can feel extremely anxious about things other people may appear to take in their stride. This is because we perceive the world differently to neurotypical people because our brains are wired differently – we are neurodiverse.

Autism is perceived in a number of different ways by autistic people. Some see it as a neurological developmental disorder – a medical model of disability which entails assessment, diagnosis and follow-up support. Others see autism from a more sociological perspective, one that is based on identity and culture – sometimes involving self-identification and the emphasis on difference rather than deficit. They highlight the promotion of 'autistic-strengths' but are not necessarily against assessment, diagnosis and follow-up support. For some of us, our understanding of autism lies somewhere in between these two perspectives. It is neither a disorder nor a cultural identity, but part of our make-up that can be disabling or enabling depending on the context we find ourselves in. As you continue to read through this anthology, you will see how some of these perspectives are reflected in the contributors' accounts.

Just to complicate things further, autism is also what is known as a spectrum condition, i.e., we have a range of abilities in the area of executive functioning, language processing, verbal ability and the capacity to live independently. Our autism may manifest in different ways. I'd like to borrow the metaphor of the elephant in the room from Buddhist teachings to illustrate the spectrum aspect of autism further. Do you know the story of the blindfolded people in a room with an elephant? One person feels the trunk and says an elephant is long and thin. Another feels its ear and says an elephant is wide and flat, and so forth. Whichever part of an elephant you happen across when wearing a blindfold will shape your view of the nature of an elephant. It is the same with autism. Some autistic people are non-verbal, some have a learning disability and others might be challenging to those that care for them. Some are non-speaking, i.e., a person who has verbal language in their thoughts but just does not speak (either through choice or because of language processing difficulties). Others may be very educated and yet socially challenged, preferring to isolate themselves and work in occupations that provide a degree of autonomy. Although some autistic people do work and have families, others live alone or with parents, finding it difficult to access work opportunities and sustain long-term relationships. A significant number of autistic adults do not get as far as being diagnosed and so do not access appropriate services. They, too, often don't succeed in accessing education and employment. Making friends or finding life partners is difficult and they may lead very isolated lives. Autism affects us all in different ways and it's not always obvious that we are autistic. But we do have certain things in common.

- Difficulties with understanding the neurotypical rules of social interaction. The world can seem a very confusing and bewildering place. We are often found on the periphery of groups, finding it difficult to make eye contact and interpret non-verbal communication.

- Our emotional responses can sometimes appear faster or slower, or more, or less, visible, than most people might expect. We also have a tendency to shut down and withdraw, or melt down and get distressed, when we feel overwhelmed by other people or a social situation. Our ability to regulate our emotions can also be limited. This can cause us to be reactive, rather than taking time to think before we respond. Other times, we can take much longer to respond emotionally because we need longer to process information. This, at times, creates the impression we lack empathy.

- 'Special interests' in which we can get very absorbed,

sometimes to the exclusion of social relationships and the demands of everyday life. Our tendency to 'info-dump' – which is to spend a lot of time talking about our special interests – can often be difficult for other people to deal with.

- A direct way of communicating with people that can be at odds with social expectations in some cultures. Our lack of ability to engage with other people may also be, at times, due to our lack of social imagination and not having a sense of how others might be feeling as a result.

- Moral and ethical in our approach to personal relationships and work issues, which can carry many benefits but can be off-putting for some people. But this, of course, does not mean that we always behave morally and ethically. We often speak up on issues of social injustice and get involved with people and movements that challenge inequality.

- Resistance to change, relying a lot on routine and feeling overwhelmed by sudden or unexpected changes. These kinds of changes can be the triggers for shutting down and isolating, or melting down and reacting angrily.

- Many of us put a lot of effort into masking our autistic traits, or as some say, 'pretending to be normal'. This can be exhausting and contribute to our need for longer recovery periods than might be expected, e.g., particularly after social events. Autistic burnout is not uncommon for us.

- Heightened senses, which while difficult to handle in many of the environments of modern life, are also a source of joy and appreciation.

The above list is not exhaustive, but it can be challenging and exhausting to live with if you are autistic! And so, it's not surprising that autism is often accompanied by degrees of depression and anxiety that further compound our social interaction difficulties.

We do have our strengths, you may be relieved to hear. For example, some autistic people, as well as having the potential to be kind and loyal in personal relationships, are good at:

- learning information and logical thinking

- working in academic areas such as science, engineering and mathematics (this may be a stereotype, and perhaps related to the view of 'male autism')

- remembering facts for a long period of time

- precision and paying attention to detail

- punctuality, reliability, following rules and adhering to routines

- concentrating for long periods of time, particularly with special interests

- direct, clear and honest communication

- spotting and naming injustices and inequality and speaking up on behalf of those they affect. This is sometimes associated with a strong sense of compassion and a commitment to work for the benefit of others.

Whatever our circumstances, difficulties or strengths, just like some neurotypical people, we can all find life a struggle. Autistic people can use lots of time and energy masking our autistic traits. We are always trying to understand what is going on because we often feel that we don't fit in anywhere, have difficulties connecting with people, and them with us, and end up feeling lonely and confused.

Buddhism can offer a way of helping us make sense of our inner world and the social world around us by providing a logical conceptual framework for life. This plays to our need for logical explanations and certainty. Meditation and mindfulness can help alleviate our experiences of confusion and anxiety by providing practical solutions. But by going further and understanding what the Buddha taught, with regular practice we can actually transform our suffering into experiences of wellbeing and happiness.

ABSENT VOICES

It is inevitable that any anthology of personal accounts of lived experiences will have voices absent from its pages, and this anthology is no different. When writing about dual identities such as autism and Buddhism, it would be easy to keep things simple and not take into account other identities such as Lesbian, Gay, Bisexual, Queer and Transgender (LGBTQ), Black and Indigenous People, People of Colour (BIPOC), and Asian people. Although within these pages there is evidence of some of the contributors aligning with the above identities, there is no submission that is written primarily from these perspectives. The absence of submissions from people who primarily identify as LGBTQ, BIPOC or Asian is a loss to this anthology.

There are complex factors that may have been at play here. Autism is less recognized by individuals, families and communities in BIPOC and Asian populations. And when autism *is* recognized, access to assessment and diagnostic services may be restricted for either financial or cultural reasons. Some families and communities accept and manage autistic people's needs internally without the need, or because of lack of trust, of external agencies. So, was reaching out to, for example, black autistic Buddhists like looking for the proverbial needle in a haystack? Further exploration of this question is beyond the remit of this book. However, there is a definite need for this issue to be explored further. My hope is that by raising the question here, it will lead to the voices of diverse communities such as LGBTQ, BIPOC and Asian autistic Buddhists being heard in a future anthology.

AUTHENTIC VOICES

'Lived experience' is a genre of writing that, as the name suggests, draws on our personal experiences rather than an academic or third-person interpretation of the matter in hand. There are already many examples of 'lived experience writing' in both the literature on autism and on Buddhism. I think that this anthology fills a gap between these two catalogues and adds to our understanding of the lived experiences of autistic people who are practising Buddhists.

Writing about one's own lived experiences for public consumption is not easy. Sharing writing in this way requires a degree of courage and discernment on the part of the writer and a responsibility on the part of the editor. When we tell our stories to other people, we make conscious or unconscious choices about what we share and who we share with. There are things that we will talk about easily and freely with pretty much anyone, but then there are other things that we might share with only a small group of trusted friends or family members. Very personal information may only be shared with a supportive professional or a very close friend, and then there are other things that we just don't talk about to anybody. There is no doubt that the contributors to this anthology will have made these kinds of choices. With some of the first drafts that were submitted, it was evident that the pieces had been developed from an initial draft of therapeutic writing. With this came a degree of responsibility for me as the editor to balance the need for you, the reader, to hear an original voice against my duty of care to the contributors.

When I started reaching out to potential contributors, I openly shared information about my background in Buddhist practice and my life as an autistic person, and some of the difficulties and successes in both these areas of my life. I invited autistic Buddhists into a space where they could feel safe enough to share as much as they felt able to. This approach was followed up in subsequent Zoom conversations and a collaborative editing process which sometimes covered up to as many as four drafts. My responsibility as an editor was also to balance the integrity of the writing that was submitted to me with the demands that I knew would be made by the publishing process, and eventually you, the end recipient. I hope that we have achieved this and that the following, often open and moving, accounts will be of benefit to all. By the way, in order to maintain the linguistic integrity of the authentic voices you are about to hear, UK or US use of English has been applied appropriately to each contribution during proofreading.

Apart from an account from Jessica Woodford that illustrates that not all autistic people come to Buddhism as adults, the majority of the other contributors to this anthology are autistic adults who are practising Buddhists (Lucy Liu and Joy Tober are parents, and Dena Rashkover is a teacher). The accounts are wide and varied. They have not been placed in any particular order, so as not to impose a structure and to help you keep an open mind as you read each individual submission. I hope you will be able to read them in a meandering, exploratory way.

Themes vary from the basics of Buddhist practice and how this can help us to improve our mental health and emotional wellbeing, to the benefits (and difficulties) of sangha and how these spiritual communities can provide autistic people with a sense of community – and real spiritual friendship and support. Buddhist precepts also feature strongly as a guide to life. The individual accounts are followed in the appendices with information about organizations and resources that will help you research autism and Buddhism further. Whether you are a Dharma teacher looking to develop your autism sensitive practice or an autistic person wishing to explore the opportunities for Buddhist practice further, you should find something of interest to help you on your way.

As you read through this anthology, you will come across mention of suicidal thoughts and self-harm, and accounts of confusion, uncertainty, anxiety and anger. But there are also lighter moments as we read about the pleasures of eating Chinese dumplings and the adventurous rescue of two turkeys from Christmas! And, as you would expect, there are many examples of the positive impact of Buddhist practice on the contributors' confidence, sense of self and overall wellbeing.

The penultimate contribution in this anthology has been written by Joy Tober, the mother of an autistic daughter who is also the administrator of a Zen Buddhist temple. Joy's account has been included to give you an idea of what life is like in just one of the thousands of Buddhist centres around the world, and what the opportunities for you might be if you were fortunate enough to find a similarly welcoming centre in your neighbourhood.

But, first off, let's hear from Louise Woodford, an autistic woman, and the mother of an autistic teenager, who was fortunate enough to meet a Buddhist monk face to face for a three-hour conversation about the Dharma. Her account tells us about some of the difficulties she has experienced, and still experiences, as a result of being autistic in a neurotypical world. She then goes on to narrate the story of how her newfound knowledge of the Dharma inspired her to change her life for the better.

CHAPTER I

How an Encounter with a Buddhist Monk Started My Journey to Wellbeing

LOUISE WOODFORD

I've always felt that I don't fit in anywhere. As a child, despite having a kind and well-intentioned family, I felt lonely and confused, I couldn't connect with people and nobody seemed to want me around. This awareness first emerged at preschool and has stayed with me for most of my life. I'd watch the other toddlers playing together and wonder, how do they do that? Throughout my school years, I felt isolated, misunderstood, and had come to expect the inevitable torment and rejection that came whenever I tried to make human connection. I eventually became defensive, untrusting, suspicious of everyone. Like many teens, my tongue was sharp, and I had an answer for everything. My temper was FIERCE – we didn't call it a meltdown then. My dad often joked that I could have an argument in an empty room. But he was right. There was an ongoing war inside my head. A constant monologue of internal ranting, filling my mind with negativity. Defending myself from all directions, firing the first arrow, just in case anyone decided to fire at me. I was vulnerable on many levels; desperate for human connection, while simultaneously defending myself from attack. I clung tightly to my pride and my opinions – I was exhausted all the time. I only ever wished to be accepted by people. I felt such compassion for people, I wanted to love and take care of people, I longed to be a good friend to somebody. I just didn't know how.

Aged 30, I couldn't cope anymore. I was now married to a very patient and understanding husband, I had a baby girl and co-owned a business with my brother. I was healthy. I had a loving family and a comfortable house, and, thankfully, being a mum turned out to be the best job in the world for me. However, the internal conflict continued to rage. I had a few public meltdowns – which was new for me as my masking abilities were accomplished. One day I sat outside a mother-and-baby group in floods of tears, shaking uncontrollably, seemingly paralysed, I just couldn't go in. I called my mum, who collected me from the carpark. She took me to her house and helped me to recover – with the help of a little Valium I might add. I knew it was time to seek help.

Sitting bolt upright in the doctor's office, with the usual stern expression on my face, I mentally prepared to present my case as to why I needed some medication to help me cope with some 'temporary stress'. However, what the doctor did next caused me to melt all over again, but this time with a strange feeling of relief. She quite simply put down her pen, took off her glasses and slowly turned her chair to face me. And with eyes of compassion, she listened. She just listened. 'I don't know what's wrong with me,' I blurted out. 'I have everything I could possibly want.' I sobbed between syllables and avoided her eye contact. I continued, 'I feel so ungrateful to be complaining like this.' Stimming like crazy and rocking backwards and forwards, I explained how, despite my privileged life, for some reason I couldn't cope with life anymore. It made no sense.

Prescription in hand, I walked to the local chemist. As I passed the shop next door, I noticed a leaflet advertising a meditation class. *Be calm and stress free* (or words to that effect). I remember stopping and urging myself to 'just try', what have I got to lose? I wrote down the details, turned around and went home.

The next night I found myself in a dark, old building in our local town centre. I wandered through the corridors, dubiously searching for the friendly bunch of meditators who were going to reveal the secret of a happy life. But I only heard silence. Having checked all the empty rooms on the ground floor, I very nearly left and went home. But, instead, I climbed a creaky old staircase. It was dark up there, and I was slightly nervous as to what on earth I was getting myself into this time. Yet, at the top of the stairs, just inside an open doorway, sat a cheerful looking monk. He welcomed me kindly with his big smile and warm, comforting northern accent. I was taken aback – I hadn't expected to see an *actual monk*! Not in this town! I sat down and waited for everyone else to arrive. Except they never did. So, for the next couple of hours, I sat there alternating beautiful meditation and deep conversation with a *real* Buddhist monk.

Everything I believed until that evening was shaken up and left to resettle in quite a different order than it was before. This kind monk spoke of acceptance, compassion, love, letting go of my opinions, accepting defeat and offering the victory to others. These words and phrases were not in my vocabulary and sounded particularly weak and puny to be frank. However, I LOVE logic, no... in fact, I *NEED* logic – and, strangely, the monk's explanations, although they challenged my perceptions, made perfect, logical sense. I was extremely interested. He seemed to lay the path of happiness right there before me and it was surprisingly rational – obvious even. Of course, one of the perks of being the only person in the class was I was free to argue. Shamelessly I doubted everything... 'But I'll be treated like a door mat...', 'But what if a person did this to me...', 'What about murderers...', 'Have compassion for him... no way?!', 'Surely I have the right to be angry about...' Despite my ignorant and slightly haughty manner, the patient, jolly, old monk looked upon me with loving eyes. He understood... deeply.

He suggested that we meditate with his guidance. The experience I had during meditation that evening... well, I'm not sure there are words to describe it. There was no up, no down, no sense of direction and no awareness of my body and surroundings – just the most peaceful, serene, empty-like space. The *only* awareness during that meditation was that monk's voice (which seemed to be all there was) penetrating my mind for those precious few minutes. That was my first experience of meditation.

During this private, precious Dharma teaching, the monk shone light onto the source of my suffering. And for that evening I had clarity. I left that building as light as a feather. Absolute relief came over me, a weight had been lifted, and for a little while, I was totally satisfied, completely content, for the first time in my life.

I couldn't help but go back for more Dharma. Every week I returned (to a bigger class now) and every week I was blown away by the simplicity and the truths that had been right here my whole life, but that I couldn't previously see. Holding, no *grasping tightly*, at the secret that no one else seemed to know, I couldn't wait to tell everyone. They will be so pleased to learn the secret of how to be happy!

How wrong I was. My clumsy, unskilful approach to spreading the Dharma just made my family and acquaintances even more uncomfortable in my presence. I certainly tried my absolute best to force Dharma down everyone's throat, but evidently my efforts were not appreciated. To give you a little more background here, I struggle with social chit-chat. I'm improving, but back then I would either be quiet in company (and appear awkward and rude) or 100% focused and in deep conversation about my latest 'special interest'. On this occasion it was the Dharma. I unknowingly distanced myself from people even more.

But thanks to Buddhist teachings, I can now recognize and control this tendency to info-dump, and I can find conversational balance. But it still takes restraint as I allow the thoughts to disperse and remember not everything I think must be said. It still takes quite intense concentration and I find it tiring to maintain for any length of time.

My new life of compassion and peace brought new friends through joining a local sangha. I had a more positive outlook, and I was happy. I wholeheartedly, religiously lived Dharma day by day for almost a decade. However, my few neurotypical friendships outside of the sangha were short-lived. The world still seemed to agree that there was 'something wrong with my brain' and that I was 'a difficult person to get along with'. The 'helpful' advice that hurt me most was that 'I act like I'm better than everyone and so people feel they can't live up to my high moral standards'. Even as a good, peace-loving, moral citizen I still wasn't accepted. I simply could not fathom what I was doing wrong. I didn't want to make people feel uncomfortable; I didn't feel better than anyone. I only wanted to cherish, to love and to help. But how?

I stopped seeing anyone outside of my sangha. People there expected nothing from me. I didn't have to remember their birthdays, call them every week for a chinwag or babysit their children. That's what neurotypical friends and family wanted from me, and I would have loved to give in that way. I did try, but my neurotypical friends didn't realize the difficulties and the anxieties I have with those things. I can't blame them for not understanding as

I mask so well. They wouldn't know how something that comes so naturally to them can cause me such difficulty.

Meanwhile, I loved Dharma, I loved meditation and everyone in my sangha was friendly. I had only loving feelings towards every member, for everyone in my life for that matter. By meditating daily on compassion I'd even found absolute peace towards those who had harmed me. Yet for all those years while I was going to the Dharma centre and chatting with people, I still struggled. Sitting in proximity with everyone there was at the same time extremely uncomfortable and sometimes unbearable. And I didn't understand why. I used to think, 'I *really* like these people, I *want* to connect with them, so why can't I? Why can't I relax in their company, why do I always want to run away?' I also felt that I was the troubled and most selfish member of our sangha. I was the member who was beyond help and who always blurted out the most ignorant comments that seemed to exit my mouth in quite a different way than I had intended. All the 'senior students' were expected to help run the centre. We'd all muck in together making the tea, cooking meals and clearing up the plates. Yet due to my executive functioning issues, I mostly avoided this. Paranoid at appearing lazy, I'd make my excuses. I was as much help in the kitchen as a chocolate teapot. I thought that I was the one who no one would be friends with, given the choice. At the end of many a session I'd go home and spend hours lying in bed. I was unable to move or open my eyes. I felt nauseous and my head throbbed. I was used to this exhaustion happening after I socialized with anyone for more than a couple of hours. Later, I'd read messages in our sangha social media group of how 'wonderful today's session was' – and I'd message to agree. It *was* wonderful, but secretly I'd struggled in ways that I knew weren't 'normal' and wouldn't be understood. 'Are they all wearing a mask like me?' I wondered. 'Are they all pretending to be sociable too?'

I asked myself, 'When having a conversation, do they *also* feel like a fish out of water, waiting to breathe again? How do they make such warm friendships?' I loved hearing Dharma teachings, so why did I dread next week's session? I watched people getting on so well together and thought, 'Look at them, no one treats me like that.' I noticed that they were like this even with new people. It didn't seem to take long for them to get to know each other. I would listen to their conversations, which were almost musical – they went up and down in beautiful rolling tones. In contrast, I was told that I sounded like a Victorian headmistress and I needed to be 'more Miss Honey, less Miss Trunchbull'. 'But I *am* inside,' I used to think. 'It just doesn't come out that way! I don't understand how I can feel such love, such compassion, such warmth for people, yet be totally incapable of showing it!'

My frustrations got the better of me on many occasions and I would decide not to see anyone anymore. This has always happened at the point when I feel pressured to teach meditation classes or facilitate meetings – which I'm inevitably asked to do – probably because my mask is so believable. They say there's 'no pressure', but I know the class won't go ahead unless I agree, then I'm overcome with guilt thinking of all those people I'm depriving of Dharma. My dream is to teach peace and mindfulness to young people, to all those autistic kids suffering at school or at home – I'd love nothing more than to help them, and I know I'm more than capable, if only I could find some way to be 'myself' in the presence of people. It's my secret wish in life – but I'm still working out how I'm going to make that happen. So, I'd silently wish the sangha well, I'd wish them love and happiness, then leave. Time and time again I'd withdraw from sangha, from everyone. I didn't tell them why as they wouldn't understand or even believe this unlikely story. And even if they did believe me what could they do? Nothing.

I'd never told anyone, sangha or otherwise, the truth about why I always ran away.

When I was in my late 30s, my eight-year-old daughter was diagnosed with autism. She was practically mute outside of our close family circle and seemed to have no interest in social interaction. Many social situations, especially school, were traumatic for her. It was a long struggle that I recognized well, and we eventually made the decision to home-educate her. It was as though I was the only person who could understand her and allow her to truly be herself. It was at this time that I realized *maybe* autism was the reason for my own struggles. I felt that if only I had a name for my troubles, I'd be able to face them, understand them and help myself to heal. I arranged an autism assessment and passed all three sections with flying colours! I remember feeling relieved at the time and thinking, 'I'm not "wrong", I'm not "broken", I'm just autistic.' I began to embrace my difference and help my children to do the same. The generic image of female autism fitted my personality so well. I could suddenly see the wood for the trees and finally understood how I could feel uncomfortable, even when I was surrounded by kind sangha.

Through the home-education community, we were able to connect with other families who had similar school stories to our own. I also found that where there was an autistic child there was invariably an autistic parent too. I soon made a network of friends and acquaintances with whom I deeply identified. We'd embrace each other's traits and idiosyncrasies, offer help and advice, and understand each other's social needs (or lack of). We were able to give each other the space we needed. I was previously blinded by confusion caused by constant rejection, not fitting in and the way people would treat me *this* way, and everybody else *that* way. But now, at least I had a name for it, at least I could embrace it and try to move on. And I have moved on.

It's been years since I've been close to a meltdown. I've learned how to recognize the overwhelm *way* before it becomes too big for me to handle. I can take care of the spark and transform it gently before any flames appear. I'm also learning to notice my fixations without engaging with them so strongly. Teachings on attachment and impermanence make this so much easier to achieve. My words and actions often don't represent what's in my heart, at least not in a socially acceptable way, but with mindful practice that's improving. I don't think autism is limiting me as a Buddhist anymore. I think it's helping me to be free of my perceptions, opinions and desires. I was limited when I felt like the world was against me, and now I try to keep an open mind. By not always believing what I think, I've often proved my perceptions to be deceptive.

This even works for the perception of being autistic. It's a label that functions for me in daily life but I'm careful not to get caught up believing that's inherently who I am. Also, by letting go of my once tightly held opinions, I'm slowly gaining a better understanding of the viewpoint of others and can therefore empathize with them. I still have the tendency to want to fix everything, teach everyone what I know and show them what they're doing wrong. But with mindfulness I'm acknowledging the possibility that maybe *my* perception is wrong. Maybe people just need to be listened to.

With daily meditation practice, I notice how much more content I have become. I've nurtured an acceptance of myself just as I am. I'm appreciating the interdependent nature of self and others and understand that we are not separate. I enjoy being free and being at one with the world – peacefully. Whenever I am able to live mindfully like this, any despair and confusion I might have experienced before (e.g., due to my views being challenged) simply cease to arise. The positive results of my Buddhist practice have given me faith in the practice, which inspires me to continue.

Buddhism has stretched my mind. It enables it to open easily, accept change, adapt and let go. I feel safe and protected. I know that with Buddhist wisdom and some effort, I can transform any adversity into the peaceful path. This will be a lifetime of learning, of course. I'm still uncomfortable socially. I still often make mistakes, so find myself avoiding social situations. But I'm only just beginning my journey – I'm aware of that. Most importantly though, there is no enemy now, no one to blame.

For me, the best thing about Buddhist teachings is that the more I practise, the more peaceful I become. And the more peace I can spread to others, the more peace I hope we can collectively offer to the world. And what's more, my literal-thinking, logic-loving autistic brain is delighted, because these teachings make perfect, logical, scientific sense.

CHAPTER 2

'Being Peace'

Buddhism Through the Eyes of an 11-Year-Old Autistic Girl

JESSICA WOODFORD

When I was a baby, my mummy became Buddhist. As I grew up, I saw my mummy meditating in the mornings, so meditation has always been normal for me. When I was eight years old, I had a strong wish to learn about Buddhism too. I wanted to be happy.

Until that time, I had been at school. I wasn't diagnosed with autism then, but I feel like I was different from the other children. At school, it was like I wasn't me. It was like I was being coded like a robot. When I look back, I can't remember any feelings other than feeling sad. I only remember my actions, robotic, like I was coded to blend in. Sometimes I would manage to ask people in my class if I could play with them, but they would act very differently, like maybe they didn't really want to play or speak to me. If I spoke to them at all, they would act strangely. My teacher put me into a club called 'Talk Boost', for the quiet children. I don't think I needed help to talk though. I could talk at home. I just needed to feel comfortable, so I could be myself.

Once, when I was four, our class was making paper toothbrushes. The teacher showed me how to make them – we had to draw round a paper template of a toothbrush, cut it out and then decorate it. I must have misunderstood because I started decorating the template by mistake. When I was finished, I showed it to the teacher. But she shouted at me. She said I had let the whole class down because there was only one template left. I was so shocked and shaken and inside I cried and cried, tears kept coming from my eyes. From then on, I was totally petrified of being told off again. I tried my best to do everything right from then on. I think this caused a fear in me, that remains even now.

After this day, I wanted to talk but I couldn't, the words wouldn't come out. I also never smiled, laughed or cried – even if I hurt myself; I never showed any emotion at all. I was just seen to be the quiet shy girl, but I wasn't shy, I was stuck. Stuck to talk, like the words were stuck in my throat, and eventually, the whole experience of school made me too scared to talk at all.

When I got home from school, I felt so relieved. However, because I had been holding my emotions in all day, at home they all came out. Usually over something little, I had a meltdown. I think I needed something to trigger my emotions so I could release them.

I don't have meltdowns anymore, probably half because I don't have to hold my emotions in anymore and half because I have learned how to take care of my feelings, through Buddhist teachings.

Mummy did meditations with me at night when I was at school. We did loving-kindness meditations, we sent love to everyone in the family, my teachers, classmates and all the animals and people throughout the world. We also did meditations to help me feel relaxed and brave. That made me feel happier and more comfortable. I still do those meditations now. By meditating I know that there is a place inside of me that is safe. No matter what's happening around me, or how people treat me, I can always go inside of my mind and find peace.

When I was eight years old my mummy decided to take me out of school, so I became home-educated. I was so happy not to be in school anymore. I wasn't coded anymore. I was myself, every day. I remember going out more, camping, to drum circle, forest school, we visited castles and other places – I felt free. Mummy and I meditate with sangha on the internet every day. Mummy helps me understand the teachings, she says I help her too! I like the teachings and meditations where I can be one with Buddha. It makes me feel safe because Buddha isn't a person out there waiting to be found. Buddha *is* the peace inside me.

I consider myself to be confident. Although other people don't view me as confident. I think some other people see confidence as being loud and bold, and I am neither. I wouldn't want to change though. Being loud and bold, I feel, wouldn't be very peaceful.

Nowadays, I still only speak when I need to, and I would never say anything unkind or dishonest. People view that as unusual and ask me why I don't speak much. The answer is, there is often no need to speak. People don't generally understand that about me; however, sangha understand. I like having sangha friends as they are Buddhist too and don't pressure me to do or say anything I don't want to.

My best friend is my brother Harry, because I can be relaxed with him and he is calm and kind. At home we all try to have respect for one another, we are happy and I feel content at home. But I remember a time when my little brother and I had an argument. I felt stressed so decided to sit down with my Avalokiteshvara statue for a while and remembered my compassion. I soon decided to say sorry to my brother and I gave him a cuddle. This made my brother and I feel much better.

I still feel a little bit different from other people, although I don't mind that. I've never understood how to make a friendship. I know friends always call each other and want to be together, and they want to chat so much, but how can there be so much to talk about? I'm trying to understand. Sometimes if I am in a bigger group of people, I don't speak at all, so I get pushed out by all the people standing around. I don't know what to do in that situation. I feel like there is something stopping me connecting to people but I just can't understand what it is. Sometimes I get extremely attached to a certain object such as a teddy or an animal. Maybe this is because I feel like I really need to have a strong connection with *something*? Because I cannot connect with friends or people, I feel I need to connect with something else. I wonder if the feeling I get with animals is how neurotypical people feel about each other. I find it much easier to socialize with animals too, because I feel more comfortable around them. They don't expect me to keep chatting. I do talk to animals, but I can talk more mindfully to them.

I've always had strong interests. For example, one of my main interests has been turkeys. One day I watched a video of a pig named Esther who had a friend turkey called Cornelius. From then, I loved turkeys! I realized turkeys are usually seen as food, not living beings. I didn't want them to be eaten anymore. I begged my mummy for almost a year, pleading to rescue a turkey from being eaten. My mummy said, 'Sorry, but we can't have a turkey in the garden!' From then on, almost everything I did was about turkeys. I would write stories about turkeys, I would draw turkeys, talk about turkeys, I even raised money to buy a turkey from the farmer – alive instead of dead. I wore a rainbow-coloured turkey hat every day, on which I sewed a turkey face. I was desperate to rescue at least one turkey from being eaten!

On 4 December 2017, Mummy agreed to let me meet a turkey, as I'd never seen one in real life before. So, we did. A free-range farmer kindly allowed us to visit the turkeys. I was shocked to see the 4000 turkeys squished into two barns.

The farmer said that all the turkeys would be gone by tomorrow, but we tried not to look sad! Now Mummy wanted to rescue a turkey too. So, we asked the farmer if we could come back to the farm the next day before the truck came to pick them up, to take two turkeys alive. He agreed. At 9am the next morning, we arrived at the farm. I turned away as the farmer hooked the turkeys by the neck and swung them upside down by the legs. I had to turn away because it was hard to see the turkeys being treated like that. They were frantically flapping their wings, trying to get back up the right way. They looked so scared; it was unbearable for me to watch.

Of course, the farmer wasn't going to give them away for free, so with the money I had raised, I paid the farmer and then we went home with two very scared and confused turkeys in the back of the car. Mummy and I didn't like giving money to that industry. But I think our turkeys (Holly and Ivy) are glad that we did. At least those two turkeys were now going to be safe. And since then, they have touched the compassion of so many people. After they had settled into their new shed, we realized how affectionate turkeys are, they really love humans! They follow me around, and whenever I go near them, they lay down for cuddles, and will even tuck their heads under their wings and meditate with me.

I don't feel angry towards the people who do eat turkeys. That wouldn't help. Buddhism has helped me to stay peaceful about that because I know it might just be because their family eats turkey as their tradition and they don't know any different. They could be driven by their attachment and desire thinking that eating the turkey is making them happy. I know how it feels to have desire for something. It's a strong feeling. They may not be able to get out of the habit. I can help farm animals by not eating them myself and spreading peace and letting people know (if they want to) about the farm animal problem.

Without Buddhism I think my strong interests would have overtaken me. My mind got stuck to my interests like glue. It was like my interest was grabbing hold of me and making me so restless – like the interest was the only way I could be happy, and I just couldn't take a break from it. But Buddhism helps me to keep this feeling under control and let go. I would have believed that my happiness was coming from turkeys and my other interests. But with Buddhism, I now understand my happiness comes from having a peaceful mind. I wish I could stop the suffering of farm animals and mass deforestation, and stop people polluting the planet and hurting each other. So recently, I did a Buddhist retreat on peaceful activism and how to be a peaceful activist. If I want to help the earth, the environment and animals, first I need to be peaceful within. Sometimes people call me an 'eco warrior'. I wouldn't call myself an 'eco warrior' because I find that it sounds like I am fighting. If I get angry about deforestation for example, it is only going to make me want to harm the people who cut down the trees. I will even harm myself, making myself upset and overwhelmed. And that isn't going to stop deforestation from happening. I need to think of a way to solve the problem with a peaceful mind and that way I won't be harming anyone. We are the earth, so if we fight with, or even *for*, the Earth, we are fighting with ourselves. I think what the eco warriors are doing is still good of course. But I'm not a warrior myself. It takes all different people to help the planet. I really admire people like Greta Thunberg, David Attenborough, Dara McAnulty and all the other activists. They really inspire me. After the retreat, I wrote a love letter to the Earth:

Dear Mother Earth,

You support all life and you give me happiness. I have taken so much from you and I have not given much back. I know you are suffering. I will do my best to help and heal you. We humans have harmed you in many ways and I am sorry.

I know you are here for us and I want you to know that I am here for you.

*When I walk outside, I see all the beautiful things that are you. When I look at a flower, I see you say hello to me. And when I hug a tree, I know I am hugging you. You are **wonderful**.*

Thank you for being there. I don't have to worry because wherever I go, no matter what, I am with you.

All my life. I will not harm you and I will help to heal you.

Jessica

I love walking in nature. I love trees, flowers and wildlife, and I think walking meditation is the perfect way to be with them. I think about how the network of fungi underneath the trees connect, how the trees can therefore communicate with each other and help each other grow without needing to speak. I *can* speak to people. If someone asks me a question, I *can* answer. If I have a question, I *can* ask it. I only wish people would have less expectations of me to chat. I wish they would allow me to sit quietly, so I can have time to process their words and think about what I am going to say. I'm not being 'rude' or 'miserable' when I am quiet, I still feel friendly towards people and I'm still happy. I wish more people could understand this. I'm glad sangha understand.

CHAPTER 3

Calm in the Eye of the Storm

How Buddhism Helps with Relationships,
Social Interactions, and Sensory Overload

DANIELLE HALL

I was not in the best place mentally or spiritually when the pandemic happened in 2020. There were so many awful things going on in the world prior to the outbreak and I lost faith in the God that I grew up loving. I was relieved that I got to take a break from the stress of person-to-person interaction with the stay-at-home order, but that break also deepened my mistrust of other humans. I acquired a sudden fear of death that had not previously been a part of my daily anxieties. I had previous exposure to Eastern philosophies through my yoga training, but prior to my Buddhist practice I had only meditated superficially, and I didn't really understand why I was meditating or what I was supposed to be doing during my sit.

One evening prior to the pandemic I had wandered into a little bookshop in town and found a small book with boxing gloves on the front, and the title was *How to Fight* by Thich Nhat Hanh. The idea of fighting really spoke to me because that is what I felt like I was doing, fighting for survival. I was experiencing regular meltdowns due to overstimulation and the storm of thoughts that raced through my mind constantly it seemed. I started reading Thay's book, but at first the teachings did not resonate with me. I kept that book in my bag for months and at the time I was not really sure why, especially considering I could not even pronounce Thay's name. When I look back to that time, I realize that I was not ready to hear what Thay (or anyone else) had to say.

When I picked up the book again in 2020 at what I felt was a significant low point, it felt as if Thay were speaking directly to me. In December of 2020, I had the mother of all meltdowns and could not take another step forward in my life without some help. I began reading and watching everything that I could from Thich Nhat Hanh and Plum Village and again felt like the message was meant for me. I began a daily sitting practice that same month that continues today.

As a newly practicing Buddhist, I had read that it would be beneficial to my practice to have the support of other Buddhist practitioners. Finding a local sangha to be a part of was a stress-inducing endeavor as I have not had good experiences in the past with other church-type communities. I have always struggled to make friends with people in general and I just did not fit with the people within that community and always felt like an oddball. I assumed that the Buddhist community would be different, for obvious reasons, but the same as far as how the people would receive me and how I would fit in. In my experience, people not on the autism spectrum understand that a person can have autism, but they may not necessarily understand what that means for an autistic person in their daily life. Our local sangha recommends that new members work with a mentor and I thought that was a good idea also, as I had jumped into this with little experience in mindfulness and meditation. After reaching out to several people within the sangha they were able to connect me with a mentor that had previously worked as a mental health professional and had experience with people on the autism spectrum. It was important for me that whoever I worked with could meet me where I was in my suffering. My initial experience with the local Buddhist community had its challenges due to my own ignorance as well as my level of suffering at the time. But I love my local sangha and I feel fortunate that my community and Buddhist teacher are incredibly loving and supportive of my autism and my practice.

I have struggled with an anxious, busy, loud, reactive, and emotional mind for as long as I can remember. My monkey mind has run the show all of these years and I needed help with how to take control and bring myself some peace. Lack of self-worth is also a source of my suffering due to my habit energy of perpetuating the narrative that I am not good enough, and I have discovered that the Metta, or loving-kindness, meditations are incredibly beneficial for helping me cope. I am quite clever and accomplished in certain areas, but because of that I place high expectations on myself to be clever and accomplished in all areas. While rationally I understand the impossible nature of always being smart and doing well, I would still suffer when I fell short. Buddhism has made me be a kinder person to myself and encouraged me to honestly just give myself a break. The emotions associated with low self-esteem and self-worth seem all-consuming at times. I use the Metta meditations on and off the cushion because it allows me to nurture the positive seeds that are necessary when I am trying to handle difficult emotions or feeling tones. When I feel anxious, I stop and close my eyes and go through my checklist of areas that I know become tense. I come back to my breathing and imagine those areas softening and melting. I have discovered that when I relax my body it makes it much easier for my mind to relax as well. I remind myself that I am all right and recite the words, 'May I be well. May I be happy. May I be peaceful and at ease.' The Metta meditations also remind me that we all have suffering.

I admittedly have trust issues when it comes to my fellow human beings, especially when they do or say things that I feel are harmful in some way. The Metta practice has allowed me to see that people are not inherently evil, simply suffering due to their causes and conditions. This is a deep practice for me and admittedly something that may take years to grasp. But simply having the understanding that someone I find difficult is really just like me and suffers just like me has helped change how I approach stressful interactions. When I am in a difficult situation with another person or have difficult feelings towards another person, I send them Metta. In my mind I recite the phrase, 'May you be happy, healthy, safe, and free from suffering.' This practice alone has provided a lot of relief from the anxiety of interacting with new people.

Prior to my Buddhist practice, I was unaware of what was actually happening in my mind and why. I would have at least one meltdown a week due to overstimulation or stress and anxiety about something in the future. I did not realize that my emotions were being fed by the narrative that I had created behind what was happening. With that in mind, I struggle with a recurring problem that I lovingly call 'schedule derailment'. I plan everything that I am going to do for the day or for the week quite meticulously, and when something comes up that I had not planned for, it creates a lot of anxiety. I feel incredibly unsettled and worry that my beautiful schedule will simply fall apart like a house of cards because of the unplanned event.

I have since learned that if I can come back to the present and my body breath connection and focus on just this moment, my emotions are not as strong. Once I am calm, I can stop and come back to the reality that I am exactly where I am supposed to be. Everything on my list will still get accomplished, and even if I miss something, everything is still ultimately fine. Naming the emotions that I am experiencing is tricky at times as I cannot always put my finger on exactly what I am feeling. But noting that I am not doing well right now has been a tremendous help in my daily life. Normally in high emotion or stressful situations I stop speaking and go inside my mind and ruminate on all of the negative things that are happening. With my practice, I still go inside my mind, but from a place of calm so that I can take care of the emotions that are there instead of suppressing them and making them stronger.

I also have three teenage sons who are on the autism spectrum and they each have their own unique challenges. When my youngest son is overstimulated or feeling stress in a situation, he retreats into himself and stops communicating. Whereas my middle child is the opposite and will explode into a rage during periods of high stress or overstimulation. My oldest is somewhere in between and can go through periods of inward retreat and outbursts. I have struggled for many years with how to help them cope because I deal with the same reactivity and had not gained the necessary tools through traditional Western therapy. With my practice, I have learned that I must first calm myself before I can hope to calm my children. In these situations, I love to use the meditation, 'Breathing in, I calm my body. Breathing out, I calm my mind.' I use that quite frequently so that I can help my boys from a calm and rational place. My practice has not only helped me but has also given me practical strategies that perhaps my boys can use into adulthood to lessen their reactivity and ultimately their suffering.

I have discovered that my practice gives me the tools to not only quiet my body and mind, but also understand why my mind is the way that it is. I love the routine of my morning meditation and the ability that it has given me to just quiet everything down for the duration of my sit. I still frequently struggle with relationships, societal interactions, and sensory overload, but my Buddhist practice has given me hope that with continued practice I will find relief from the storm that is my reactive mind. The more comfortable I become with how and why my mind reacts the way that it does, the better equipped I will be to lessen the reactivity that creates so much of my suffering.

CHAPTER 4

True Freedom

What Buddhism Teaches Us about Difference and Acceptance

PETE GRELLA

Life can be very challenging when you are autistic. The challenges can be quite overwhelming and create intense feelings, both good and bad. The one thing that I have found to deal with this has been Buddhism. The lesson of the Dharma has been instrumental for me in dealing with these feelings. But before I tell you about how Buddhism has helped me, let me tell you a little more about me. I remember as a child looking out the window and seeing the other kids in the street playing, and asking myself why, why am I on this side of the window and how can I get to the other side? For the next several decades I asked myself the same question over and over again, why, what is going on here, what am I doing wrong? It is as if when the other kids were born, they were issued a handbook on how to interact with people that I never got. I used to think that when I die, I want an autopsy done on my brain, because I was sure that there was something different about it.

I was aware of autism, but only the non-verbal kind, and I wasn't that. I could talk, I could force myself to look people in the eye (but I didn't enjoy it), I could read obvious facial expressions, but not subtle ones. I could tell that my emotions were different from other people's. They were all or nothing. Most of the time I didn't have any, but when I did, they were overwhelming. I would wonder, as a child, if people would think me a monster if I did not cry at my parents' funeral when the time came. I would see patterns in things when other people would not and notice smells before others. I would leave a building the same way I entered, and now, when I drive to a place, that will be the only route I take when I go to that place again. I wondered why I was so alone and unable to connect with other people when I was putting myself out there as much as anyone.

I finally got the answer to that question: why? I was autistic. Autism means we have different body language and facial expressions that are seen as unfriendly by the neurotypical world. I've had people tell me that they thought there was something wrong with me because I sometimes rock back and forth when I stand. And other people have told me that this rocking makes them think that they are making me nervous and so they want to get away from me. They also say my blank facial expressions and monotone voice make a negative first impression. I don't have the same kind of ability to read neurotypical people's emotions the same way they can read each other's. I was telling a therapist once that I have empathy. When someone tells me that their dog died, I know to treat them with sensitivity. My therapist said, 'Yeh Pete, that is part of empathy, but other people actually feel what the other person is feeling.' I said, 'Are you shitting me? You mean other people can actually feel what other people are feeling?'

Imagine that you are at a party, and everyone at that party has a light bulb above their head, and that light bulb varies in intensity by what the person is feeling. I can't see that light bulb and you can't see mine. I am blind to your feelings and mine are a blank slate to you. Connections with other people are the most important thing to lead a happy life and those connections are made through emotional bridges. We are descended from people who survived by bonding with other humans. I have a desire to be with other people, but because of autism I don't have the wiring to make that happen. If you were to design a condition to rob you of your happiness it would be autism. It robs us of the emotional bridges needed to connect with humanity, leading to unhappiness. And on top of that, after robbing us of our happiness, autism will amplify whatever emotion we are feeling, making us feel even worse. It is no wonder that the suicide rate and rates of depression amongst the autistic population is many times higher than that of the general population. This is something I can very much relate to, having experienced depression and suicidal thoughts myself. But there is hope. Of all the things I've tried, or contemplated, to alleviate the suffering caused by autism, I have found one thing that helps more than any other – Buddhism.

There are many concepts in the Dharma that have made life a little bit easier on this side of the window – like the Buddhist concept of 'no-self'. Buddhism tells me that my idea of 'self' is a story created by conditioning and labels such as son, brother, computer programmer, male, straight, middle aged, American, and Los Angelino. But Buddhism tells me there is another way to be that is free of these labels. As my meditation practice has deepened, I am more able to be the consciousness that is experiencing this moment – whatever my senses are taking in here and now. I once read Eckhart Tolle's book *The Power of Now* that explores this concept further. One day after reading it, I was walking down the street noticing the flowers and the geometry of the sidewalk before me, then I noticed the feeling of the air between my body and my shirt. I had never experienced this before. Then I knew what Eckhart was talking about.

Buddhism showed me that there is another way to look at

these things, that I am not that 'self' that is always failing at relationships but just a consciousness experiencing this present moment. This has reduced the amount of pain from this by about 50%. This concept of 'no-self' has been very useful in dealing with being autistic. For example, the Buddha also talked about the 'comparing mind'. I like to say that my life moves in slow motion. Other events that happen in other people's lives seem to take forever for me. Other people seem to move in and out of relationships while I remain static, alone year after year after year. Even the frequency with which I communicate is slower than other people. I would always be comparing myself to other people wondering why they are able to achieve things, especially when it comes to relationships, and I would feel really bad about myself for being such a failure. The concept of 'no-self' balances my tendency to compare myself with others.

There are other specific consequences of autism that Buddhist concepts have helped me with, such as the Buddhist concept called 'Right View' which encourages us to develop a deep understanding of the Four Noble Truths. I sometimes suffer with what are commonly called meltdowns, when my nervous system becomes overstimulated by emotional or sensory triggers. I am a computer programmer by trade. Sometimes after writing hundreds of lines of code and processing for hours, I'll find a mistake in my program, and I have to run it again. This can lead to a meltdown, where I get so angry that I'll tense all my muscles. So, I started to acknowledge my suffering and ask myself, 'What is going on here?' I found the answer in what Buddhism calls 'attachment', one of the primary causes of our suffering. So, the question was, 'What am I attached to here?' I am self-employed and I cherish my free time. I would rather cultivate free time than make as much money as I can. When I make a mistake it cuts into my free time, and I am attached to that. I also realized that I had an unrealistic expectation that I would never make mistakes. Realizing these things as causes of my suffering mitigates the meltdowns.

Meditation has also helped in the above situation by providing me with a practical solution rooted in Buddhist practice. Viktor E. Frankl, a neurologist, psychologist, and Holocaust survivor, was reported to have said, 'Between stimulus and response there is a space, and in that space is our power to choose our response. In our response lies our growth and freedom.' When I meditate, I practice observing my thoughts and not being attached to my thoughts. I imagine my thoughts inside a bubble, and rather than being inside the bubble possessed by my thoughts, I try to be outside the bubble observing my thoughts. So now, thanks to the practice of meditation, when I make a programming mistake, and the thoughts of meltdown begin to amplify, I am now able to observe the experience and, most of the time, have the space to do something different, sit still until the sensation passes rather than giving in to it and melting down. Our thoughts are like a stream of water flowing over a rock. Over time, the water will cut a groove in the rock and the water will always flow the same way. When I react to situations with the same thoughts, that will create a connection of neurons that will fire the same way in situation after situation. When I meditate, I create new, positive neural connections. So, when confronted with the same situations, I won't always fall back into the same thinking patterns, as if a new groove has been created on the rock so the water can flow differently.

Another meditation technique that can change our thinking patterns is Metta practice. Metta practice is repeating phrases of wellbeing while we meditate, phrases like, 'May everyone be happy, may everyone be at ease.' This too can change our pattern of thinking. I first noticed this when, after years of hearing voices in my head telling me what a loser I was, one day I heard a voice that said, 'I love you.' I have a story to tell about how Metta meditation helps me. One time I went to go see one of my favorite Black Metal bands in concert. They launched into one of their signature songs and a pit broke out. I got inadvertently pulled into the pit and got knocked down. I could not get up by myself and I started to panic. People helped me up and I was OK. Now, I have a heart condition called atrial fibrillation, where my heart will beat out of control, and I start to pass out. After I was pulled from the pit I went to the back of the club, and I could sense an 'afib' happening. I started to feel nauseous, I started to feel hot, and I was getting tunnel vision and I knew I was on my way to passing out. I figured I could make it to the lobby and lay down and ride it out. So, I started to make a beeline to the lobby hoping I would get there before I passed out. Now, in the past, I would be telling myself things like, 'Why me, what's wrong with you, can't you maintain, this really sucks, you're not fit to go out.' But this time I had a different refrain: 'This is an inevitable part of my existence, this will pass, this is temporary, you will be OK, don't worry about what people think.' This was only possible because of my Metta practice. I was able to make it to the lobby and lie down and ride it out not worrying about what others may think.

Another way meditation helps me with autism is dealing with social situations. Before a social event, I used to get worried and go over, in my head, what I was going to say. Hoping I wouldn't say something that would make people not like me or trying to plan for something interesting to say so that people would like me. During the event, I would be nervous and always second-guessing myself wondering what to say. Afterwards I would evaluate myself trying to figure out what I could have done better, and if I said something that was particularly embarrassing or stupid it could haunt me for years to come. Now, we come equipped with a mind that is always functioning,

it wants to think. When we are engaged in volitional thinking for making plans our mind can be very useful. But if we
become obsessed and engage in continuous rumination our
mind can become an enemy. So, it is fine for me to think about
what I might say at a social event for a moment or two, but if
it becomes an obsession where I continuously think about it
over and over again, it is a problem. When I practice focusing
on my breath, while meditating, I learn to focus on something
other than my thoughts. After years of meditating like this, I
have been able to control the ruminations before a social event.
The same technique can be applied to after the event, where
in the past I would ruminate on my performance and how I
could have improved it and what went wrong. Again, because
of meditation, I can control that tendency.

The Dharma also helps me with enjoying social events. Buddhism teaches a concept called Right Speech, which encourages
us to be aware of the suffering that can be caused by unmindful
speech and the inability to listen to others. Before I say something, I ask myself: 'Is it true? Is it the right time to say it? Is it
helpful? Is it kind?' Right Speech steers me away from gossip
and away from speech that divides people – to speech that
brings people together. It helps me to not come from a position of one-upmanship or anger. By practicing Right Speech, I
am giving my full attention to whoever is speaking instead of
thinking about what I am going to say.

Compassion is another Buddhist concept that helps me to
mitigate the effects of my autism. I used to think that, in social
situations, small talk was a steppingstone to a more profound
discussion. If you wanted to talk about the weather, I would
hope it would lead to a discussion on the effects of climate
change on hurricane formations. When small talk did not lead
to a more profound discussion, I thought I had failed. In a doc-
umentary on autism, I saw an interview with a woman with

autism talking about small talk. She said, 'Whatever is going on in my head is far more interesting than anything you have to say to me.' I could relate to that. When I tell my neurotypical friends this they tell me I'm a jerk. This woman said that her father told her that people get energized from small talk. Like those internet games where you get points for doing something that recharges you, most people get energized from small talk. When I learned this, small talk became easier. I now view it as an altruistic venture, that I am helping people. One time the meditation center I used to go to organized a street clean-up to pick up garbage that had accumulated a block away. While we were doing it, some of the locals came out to help. One of them started talking to me. In the past, this would have been an unpleasant situation for me, but once I knew that he was benefitting from this encounter, it was much easier to engage with him more compassionately without any judgement.

I suppose the greatest benefit of Buddhism is orienting me towards how I am like everyone else, not how I am different. Ultimately Buddhism teaches us that all we are is the consciousness that experiences whatever our senses are experiencing in the present moment. This is true for all of us, no matter what our brain wiring is. My experiences may be filtered through a neurodiverse brain, but the consciousness that receives the experience is the same in all of us. Ultimately, whatever I experience can be reduced to a physical manifestation in my body. My emotions express themselves in my body. When something good happens, I feel it in my body, and I want to feel that feeling again (attachment) – so I chase that feeling. If something bad happens the feelings express themselves in my body in a particular way – and I want to run away from those feelings (aversion). Buddhism preaches equanimity, to fully accept whatever arises. If we can learn to accept whatever we are feeling (in our body) equally, then we can stop chasing what we think will make us feel good and stop running away from what we think will make us feel bad. And it's not all bad, there are a few benefits of autism – I can concentrate really well, I can really wrap my mind around something I enjoy, I know that when I listen to music, I enjoy it in a way most others do not. In fact, if I were on an island by myself, autism might be beneficial. The angst of autism comes from the friction caused by trying to fit in to a neurotypical world. Buddhism releases me from that angst. And that is true freedom.

CHAPTER 5

Dharma D'Au

Buddhism, Autism and the Path to Balance

SIAN ATKINS

A year ago, I knew next to nothing about Buddhism. These days, it is my foremost interest as I find myself inspired and comforted upon hearing the teachings, and have settled into a daily routine of sitting, walking and lying down practices, combined with frequent self-reminders (and thus, of course, forgettings) to return myself to the present moment throughout each day. Whilst I am still so new to this path – and not without anxieties, occasional overwhelms and many questions – my overriding feelings about and throughout this journey so far have been of joy, tenderness and lots of gratitude.

There are a couple of stand-out factors which enabled my Dharma discovery, as well as providing favourable conditions for supporting and nourishing my growing interest over time. First is that I found my way to Buddhist practice through autistic community and connection, which itself, owing to the coronavirus pandemic, was facilitated through online space with its numerous accessibility benefits. Second, and in the context of autistic 'intense interests', are the internal conditions of my own motivation and ability to engage with this emerging interest, and how Dharma itself may offer valuable wisdom and support in this process.

My first encounter with meditation was around four years ago, in my late 20s, following a short bout of mindfulness-based therapy. I followed the prescribed meditation routine for about a year, but found my motivation, and the frequency and lengths of sits, dwindled over time until I abandoned the practice altogether. In the years following, a vague yet persistent feeling about the value of meditation lingered in the background, but the impulse to return felt very much along the lines of 'should' rather than 'want' and didn't translate into reality.

It wasn't until summer/autumn 2020, during and following the online version of *Autscape* (a conference run by and for autistic people), that things shifted for me, and quite dramatically. Amidst the busy conference, a text thread entitled 'quieting' emerged around the intersections of autism and contemplative practices. This discussion became ongoing and subsequently led me to meeting with a couple of autist Dharma practitioners for weekly video sits and chats.

First to say, it was seeing and learning about meditation within the context of Buddhism that really ignited my interest. Before, I'd had little to no idea about this connection, and it came to make everything feel so much more meaningful than had ever been the case with my first experience. Also helpful was the gradual and gentle – whilst also satisfying and powerful – nature of sharing in this wisdom and practice with my new friends, as well as the fact of our meetings being sustained for almost a year. It felt to me very much like a case of Dharma being 'caught' rather than simply taught. I'd catch little bursts of feelings and fragrances in my heart and senses, at once softening and invigorating, which moved me to *want* to learn. Over time, my interest grew enough momentum to become self-motivating and self-sustaining, spreading out to spaces beyond our weekly meetings. I committed to solo practice, engaged with an ever-growing list of Dharma talks and books, and began attending online workshops and retreats.

It's hard to overstate the pivotal role that connecting with my new practitioner friends has had in where I am now and in my 'decision' to pursue this path. Of course, the process of encountering and entering through a Dharma door always takes place in a relational context of some sort, whether that be indirectly through something like a piece of writing, or more directly as it was for me. In my own case, I feel there were a couple of additional factors, both quite unique and fortunate, which further facilitated this process.

Most obviously, everything shared was through our shared experience of being autistic. And so there was the fact of autist affinity. Whilst not wanting to idealize autistic community (we are as diverse a group as any other), it often fosters a valuable sense of commonality and connectedness – an experience of suddenly feeling 'the same' because of one's differences – and all the more so if it is rarely encountered (autistic people being a relatively small minority). I feel our meetings also helped me to come into closer contact with my own autistic identity. As I discuss further below, I had recently experienced the loss of an intense interest in autism and an associated distancing from the identity. Buddhism in general, and connecting with autist Dharma friends in particular, has reignited some of my interest in autistic (and also queer) identity, solidarity and activism, and in some quite new and wholesome ways. It's exciting to see the inclusion of affinity groupings within Dharma spaces and it's something I hope will continue to grow, especially around disability (let alone neurodiversity within that), which is so lacking. Of course, it can seem somewhat paradoxical to be forming identity-based sangha amid teachings of not-self and absolute reality. And yet, as I have learned through attending

Rainbow (LGBTQ+) retreats, Buddhism seems well-placed, perhaps almost uniquely so, to hold this creative tension between both sides of reality – both 'there' and 'not there', both different and the same – in true middle way fashion.

This brings me to my next point, that our meetings were a place of intersecting interests and practices. Whilst Dharma took centre stage, it was always, quite naturally, filtered through our autistic embodiments, whether this was made explicit or not. There can be something quite powerful in the crossover of interests. Like the confluence of two rivers, each adds to the other, often in novel and much needed ways, given the narrower (but also in a way, wider) and hence more unique space being occupied. Examples of this for us included: an autist-focused Metta Bhavana, tracing imagined infinity symbols during walking and other movement meditations, and developing an insight dialogue practice sensitive to our autist natures (e.g., carrying no expectations around eye contact or speaking).

An additional benefit of meeting within this affinity space was our first-hand experience and innate understanding around commonly held autistic needs and preferences. This was combined with a strong sense of the particular importance of listening and accommodating around areas of difference, difficulty and conflicting access needs. Ways of enabling and reflecting this included: ensuring ample space for everyone to contribute (or not), demonstrating patience and non-judgement around differing communication styles, welcoming text contributions both in and around meetings, including comfort breaks, and friendliness towards stimming and movement more generally. Fostering such an air of openness and acceptance carries huge emotional as well as practical benefit and seems perhaps especially well-supported by the combination of Buddhist values and various aspects of autist nature and culture.

I found the context of meeting online, whilst placing some

obvious limits, provided many advantages in terms of accessibility and comfort. I had full control over my physical environment in terms of lighting (which I prefer dim) and seating (tending to involve many cushions). I could adjust the computer volume if incoming sounds were too loud, and mute my mic if I needed to make a noise (such as cough) others might find unpleasant. Although connecting via screens can in some ways feel less connected or 'real', it can also prove less sensorially or emotionally overwhelming than in-person interactions. It's easy to factor in breaks or to step away from the call for a moment for whatever reason, and there is the obvious advantage of no energy expenditure associated with having to travel to and from the space. Overall, there is a pairing of closeness and distance, which can feel like a helpful balance and compromise. In addition, the simple fact of autistic community being small and geographically dispersed makes online an especially useful, often essential, medium for us to find one another and come together.

Owing to the pandemic, I have yet to experience being in person at any Dharma space. Whilst I am excited to venture out when the time comes, I also have a few concerns about doing so. These include expectations around sitting on the floor or in a (not-so-comfortable) chair, which, due to my probably autist-related physical health and motor needs, I struggle to do for any length of time. And whilst I imagine meditation halls to be relatively tranquil places, I do wonder about potential issues with things like background noise and bright lighting. Another barrier is anxiety at entering a new space populated with unfamiliar people, and then navigating interactions, until I reach a place of feeling more settled within the environment and accustomed to the various faces. Something I found immensely helpful about meeting with my Dharma friends was the fact of us being a trio. I find 1:1 or very small group interactions much easier to manage (or alternatively, very large groups where there can be lack of pressure in invisibility), as processing differences along with anxiety can make it difficult for me to verbally contribute within medium to large sized groups. I am, however, optimistic that sanghas I intend on joining in future, both online and off, will prove welcoming and understanding places, and that my own practice will likewise help in facing anxiety with courage and kindness.

I feel it is both touching and rather telling that I came to Dharma as a direct result of meeting and connecting with practitioner friends, as well as through exploring various elements of the (online) Buddhist community more widely. Intrinsic, internally derived motivation is a common autistic trait, and a requisite along the path. It has long been a strength of mine, although in recent years I have noticed something of a turn towards and benefitting from a more socially derived motivation as well. Buddhist teachings remind me of the importance of having both: a committed and self-sufficient individual, but one who is ideally supported within, and thus supporting, a wider social web comprising sangha, spiritual friendship and an evolving sense of interdependence manifesting as ethical conduct. I hope to increasingly experience the benefits of openness to the external (which I personally feel can be quite 'fiery', as in warming but also potentially burning), whilst remaining internally balanced; and balancing with, what are to me, the more natural, cooling and calming waters of solitude and silence.

During this first year of beginning to study the Dharma, I have found it interesting to note aspects inherent to autist 'special interests' reflected in certain core Buddhist qualities, including focused attention, perseverance and intrinsic joy. For myself, however, alongside their immense value, I also recognize something of a downside in how intense interests tend to play out in my life. This centres mainly around a lack of balance and often calm, which may be partly responsible for the unfortunate fading of each one after a few years. Perhaps this is a largely inevitable process for me. And I do of course recognize a positive in this – as one door closes, another opens. However, recently, I have begun to notice how Buddhist teachings, as well as the qualities inherent to my experience of practising Buddhism, provide a relevant and potentially very helpful context when it comes to more skilfully managing interests within my life.

The first of these intrinsic qualities are *balance* and *tranquillity*. Almost all my intense interests to date have been of an intellectual language-based kind, involving sitting at a desk, reading, writing and generally working my way through as much information on a given topic as possible. Most recently this was around autism when, following a late diagnosis, I spent several years deep diving into the research literature and advocacy community. Then, quite suddenly, and coinciding with a period of social and emotional upheaval in my life, my motivation nosedived from 100% to pretty much 0%, and I abandoned most activities associated with the interest. In the couple of years since that burnout and loss of interest, I've been experiencing more fatigue than usual, heightened sensory sensitivities (including in positive ways) and an apparent turning away from engaging in text-based interests. I have found myself shifting instead towards enjoying more sensory and body-based activities, like art, music, movement and spending time in nature, which has brought both new and rediscovered sources of joy and meaning into my life. However, in a way, this represented a shift to almost the other extreme, as I didn't pick up a book and barely read or wrote anything online for well over a year.

Then, when my interest in Buddhism was piqued, I naturally found myself wanting to know more, which meant wanting to read. Yet at the same time, I felt resistance to doing so as I knew

I would quickly hit a wall of text fatigue and information satura-
tion. However, as the months have passed, I've gradually found
myself more able and willing to take in information around this
growing interest, particularly through the combined auditory
and visual format of video. I also hope to have learned from
my past experiences. Currently, I am trying to walk a balance
between the competing (but also complementary) desires of
letting myself run loose with the interest and my sense of
urgency around it, versus listening to the parts of my mind,
and especially body, which call for things like lessening, slowing
down, moving around, opening out or simply shutting off.

In a way, my lowered tolerance for information consumption
is functioning as an in-built mechanism towards moderation
and encouraging rest. In addition, I'm increasingly aware of
how Buddhist teachings around equanimity and tranquillity
can serve as useful reminders and tools for arriving at and
accepting whatever activity-to-rest ratio seems to work best
for me. It's surely no coincidence that Buddhism encompasses
both study and practice (and with the latter incorporating both
sitting still and movement), and thus has contrast and balance,
and so self-care and wellness, built in to it. Moreover, hearing
teachings about the primacy of practice over study, aspiring to
dwell beyond language or in 'don't know' mind and seeing the
body as one's very own best teacher has been great for calming
my anxieties around knowledge acquisition. I appear to have
landed on an interest which is a practice for finding more
balance and peace in relation to the interest itself, along with
everything else.

The second aspect of Dharma entirely related to my experience of balance and tranquillity is *interconnection*. As an autist,
I often experience my interests as intense, deep, detailed and
– probably related to these factors – being focused on quite
specific, sometimes niche, areas. Unfortunately, this has often

been translated as 'overly narrow' or 'idiosyncratic', with the assumption that the interest is of limited value and, in fact, rather uninteresting. Such a perspective not only brushes over the value of depth, specialized knowledge and intrinsic joy. It also ignores how many autists like me experience a process of widening out from a singular interest, through noticing connections to many other related things, both near and distant. As a result, we may come to see the entire wood precisely *because* we see that one tree so well.

An interest in Buddhism could be seen as a good, if perhaps extreme, example of this. From the outside and on a surface level, I recognize how it might appear, and so be written off, as a quite specific area of inquiry, or as something perhaps meant only for a certain group of (religious or spiritual-type) people. Indeed, this is how I viewed Buddhism to begin with, until I'd heard enough for my perspective to completely flip. Once you are *in* it, the breadth of the teachings and practices become increasingly apparent, and it comes to seem anything but narrow. Personally, I have noticed how many of my past interests interconnect and can be seen as widening out to broadly similar areas or purposes. These include various topics within the psychology of personality, relationships and wellness, around marginalized identities (of disability and queerness) and justice issues (e.g., climate change, international development). In discovering Buddhism, I have found myself revisiting parts of these old interests (e.g., autism and climate change), as well as acquiring new aspects (e.g., veganism), and seeing the relationships between them (which, of course, is a key Buddhist teaching). Whilst many of them are admittedly more easily and obviously related to Dharma than other areas might be, the Dharma itself seems to function as a sort of hub or container for connecting (as well as questioning and perhaps abandoning) a whole range of interests and pursuits. This helps to bring, in flowing infinity-symbol motion, greater interest into the practice, and, in turn, the practice more into one's interests and life.

Throughout my life I've experienced a repeating pattern of intense interests arriving, blazing and then burning out within a few years. With Buddhism, however, I am optimistic that qualities inherent to the interest itself – including tranquillity, equanimity and interconnectedness – will prove supportive in terms of the practice staying with me over the years. Through learning to bring rest to interest and interest to rest, I aspire to pause more often at the central resting place of the infinity symbol, in the here and now, with body-mind calmed, balanced and connected. And more widely, liberation – as both process and destination, personal and collective – strikes me as an ultimate and unending source of inspiration and challenge. It is in recognizing a long road ahead, as well as a wider point (around relationality, ethics and justice issues), that also draws me to this path. Balancing patience and urgency, like water and fire, I hope to proceed with a steady glow, or gentle ebb and flow, along the way.

CHAPTER 6

The Triple Jewel

How Buddhism Helps Me Manage Anxiety in Everyday Life

CHRIS JARRELL

The Triple Jewel is the combination of the Buddha, the Dharma and the Sangha that provides a refuge for those of us who have committed to studying Buddhism and following the Noble Eightfold Path. It takes me further than the secular practice of mindfulness and meditation. It enables me to feel the deeper presence of loving kindness, compassion, joy and equanimity and the possibilities for wellbeing that these qualities embrace. The Triple Jewel helps me to sense that the Buddha is still here today through his teachings and the support available through Buddhist spiritual communities. The refuge provided by the Triple Jewel is not about withdrawing from the world. It enables me to be more present in the real world through the practice of mindfulness in everyday life. It supports me in my practice, and I feel less isolated and alone. I find that the Triple Jewel provides a good counterbalance for some of the more antiso-cial and selfish aspects of my autistic self that impinge on my wellbeing and the wellbeing of others each day.

When I wake up on a good day, I notice a momentary absence of thought and I get a real sense of what being in the present moment means. This is before my mind switches on and I start to think. I notice the quietness that comes before the business of the day. Usually only for a few seconds, but enough to give me hope that it is possible for my mind to be peaceful. I am hopeful that my practice is working and that it has some use, some purpose. In those few seconds there are no feelings of anxiety, disconnect and isolation, no overthinking, worrying about the future or dwelling on the past. All consequences of my autism that visit me during the day. And so, I set my intention to be of benefit to others, which is one of the core principles of the Mahayana tradition.

On a good day, I may lie in bed for a while and observe my breath. I may even quietly recite to myself the first lines of a Plum Village chant:

May the day be well, may the night be well, may the midnight hour bring happiness too.

In every moment and every second, may the day and the night be well.

By the blessing of the Triple Jewel may we all be protected and safe.
(Plum Village, 2020, with permission)

I try and sit for 20 minutes each morning, but it doesn't always work out. If I am tired and anxious, I find it very difficult to sit and be with my feelings. So, if I don't sit formally, I look for other opportunities during the day to practise – like a walking meditation in the garden, being mindful of my breathing while I am working on the allotment or, sometimes, just making sure I take a nap and generally be kind to myself by not overdoing things. Taking time to just sit and chill.

When I do sit, I use a wooden meditation stool that has been my friend for many years. It's handmade and feels great to touch and hold. It helps to keep the weight of my body off my legs so I can sit for longer periods. I sit in my back room, which is a quiet part of the house. I have a regular space in the corner where I can sit and stare at the wall. I set my telephone timer for 20 minutes, bow to the wall and then kneel, usually with a smile of recognition that I am coming home. I begin with a breathing meditation inspired by a Plum Village guided meditation:

> *Breathing in, I know I am breathing in, breathing out, I know I am breathing out.*

I usually run through this breathing meditation three times to help me settle. I may also scan my body, from the top of my head to the tips of my toes, for aches and pains. That's important at my time of life because minor ailments can creep up on you and it's good to catch them early. I ask myself how I am feeling (because I don't always know) and check on whether there's a lot of thinking going on, usually there is! Each time I notice I am thinking a lot, I smile and try and return to my breathing. But thinking is difficult to let go of in my experience, as one thought often leads to another. My thoughts swing from branch to branch just like a monkey swinging through the trees. For example, I may notice the sound of the refuse truck turning into the street, I wonder whether I locked the back gate after putting out the bins, but then remember I couldn't because the latch is broken, and I need to go to the hardware store to buy a new one, and while I'm out I should go to the post office and send that parcel to Scotland, which reminds me that the post office closes at lunchtime today, so I'd better get a move on. I've got lots to do this morning. My mind begins a to-do list. Monkey brain, stop right there! I return to observing my breath, take a deep, slow breath, smile and let go.

> *Breathing in, I know I am breathing deeply, breathing out, I know I am breathing slowly.*

When I am sitting, if my breathing seems shallow and tight

it usually means I am feeling stressed and anxious. Practising breathing in deeply and feeling my abdomen rise, and breathing out slowly while observing my breath, helps me to relax physically, which in turn helps me to settle into my morning meditation. I may also roll my head on my shoulders or rotate my shoulders to help with this. When my breathing is shallow and tight it reminds me to look deeply into possible reasons for my stress and anxiety. Sometimes the answer is fairly near the surface and I am able to smile and let go, making a mental note to check back in with this later and see if I can alleviate the cause of my unease. For example, I may be making a Zoom call that morning and so I will need to make sure that I prepare. Note to self. But other times the answer is less forthcoming and so I resolve to write a journal entry, or talk to my wife or sister who both understand how my autism affects my mental health (and are good listeners). So, on a good day, when I am sitting, my breathing will deepen and slow down as I follow my breath, observe my thoughts, feelings and body, smile and let go.

Breathing in, I know I am calming down, breathing out, I know I am relaxing.

On a good day, as I relax into my morning meditation, I am able to sit and observe my thoughts and feelings, watching them come and go. Very much like when I am sitting on my allotment with a mug of tea staring at the blue sky, relaxing and chilling, and noticing the clouds pass by. As a cloud comes into view I try and maintain my awareness of the clear and empty blue sky beyond. I don't try too hard because that would defeat the object of calming down and relaxing. But over time it becomes easier just to notice the cloud as it passes by, rather than attach to it. Which is one benefit of my morning meditation, practising just sitting and noticing thoughts and feelings pass by without attaching to them.

Breathing in, I know I am smiling, breathing out, I know I am letting go.

On a good day, sitting staring at the wall, I am able to follow my breath, smile and let go of the thoughts and feelings passing through my awareness. The thoughts may be memories, ideas, worries and concerns about what is to come or what has occurred. And the feelings may be anxiety or anger, sometimes joy and wellbeing. Smiling and letting go is not always easy, but as my practice has deepened over the years, through regular practice, it has become easier. It has also become easier since I received my diagnosis of Autism Spectrum Disorder and I have more clarity about why I am like I am. And why I have felt so different and disconnected over the years. My Buddhist practice and my diagnosis combine to help me to be more accepting of who I am. On a good day, I can smile and let go of the feeling that I am a bad neurotypical person and accept that I am a good enough autistic person.

Breathing in, I am aware that this is the present moment, breathing out, I am aware that this is a wonderful moment.

On a good day, I sit and look at the wall and smile. My head is clear and I feel well. And when the phone alarm gently sounds and I stand and bow to the wall, I start my day feeling more relaxed and less anxious.

These days my practice is not just about sitting, walking or working meditation. Over the years I have gradually been able to practise in the moment as my day unfolds. I am more able to integrate meditation and mindfulness into my daily life. (It doesn't always work out and I have learned to be kind to myself and accept that I'm probably not going to attain enlightenment in this life!) But a case in point, just last weekend I had to go to the furniture shop to collect two new chairs that

I had ordered online. I needed them in a hurry because we had visitors arriving (and the cat had decided to sharpen its claws on two of our dining room chairs). We wanted things to look nice for our guests.

So, I drove to the shop feeling anxious because I don't find it easy going shopping. My senses are overloaded by the store lighting, the crowds of shoppers, the large choice of goods on display and the public announcements of the daily bargains to be had. I find all of this exhausting, and this was going to be on the back of a busy weekend of visitors at the house. So, I was already worried that I wasn't going to cope over the next few days. But I reassured myself that I just needed to find the right checkout and I should be in and out in minutes with my two new chairs – with just a minor hit on my emotional reserves. I found an available shopping cart and walked over to the counter. What could go wrong?

I handed the shop assistant a computer printout of my order and they turned to the computer and started tapping away, for quite a while. And then, without saying anything, and without even looking at me, they turned and disappeared into the back of the store. My expectation of customer care is that I should be kept informed of what is going on, at least be acknowledged in some way. Perhaps with a reassuring, 'I'll be back in a minute.' I have learned in situations like this to try and stay calm because I know that I am likely to get wound up and have a meltdown if things don't go the way I expect them to. (I know that this may not just be about my autism, neurotypical people may react in the same way.) Anyway, I began to get anxious about getting anxious. Maybe they had just gone to get the chairs?

While I waited, I tried to follow my breath and breathe deeply and slowly, keeping calm and relaxed, smiling and letting go. I watched other customers come and go, noticing that most of them were presenting their phones rather than computer printouts. I've never been able to make the change, I like to keep things as they are unless I am forced to change, and then I do so reluctantly. 'But maybe that's just about me getting old,' I told myself as I watched people walk away with their household items. I kind of enjoyed watching them, it's good to see people happy and being out with their friends and families.

The assistant came back with someone who had the air of 'supervisor' about them. Again, without even glancing at me, they both got involved in checking the computer, occasionally glancing at my printout. Eventually, the supervisor turned to me and said something like, 'I'm sorry but we have a problem. The truck only delivered one of your chairs this morning.'

'So can I take the one you have and come back tomorrow for the other one?' I asked.

'No,' they said. 'The computer doesn't allow that to happen. You have to have both chairs, or no chairs at all.'

By now I must have been giving them what my wife calls my John Cleese 'scary look'. Direct eye contact and intense. Before I knew it, the supervisor had disappeared out back again and the assistant had moved to another checkout and started serving other customers. I thought they had just abandoned me. I stood frozen to the spot not knowing whether to walk out or push for the one chair that I knew was in the store somewhere. I looked around at the other customers and felt the usual disconnect intensified. They seemed like they were in another world behind a transparent screen, and I felt very alone. I thought they were talking about me and judging me. I began to feel angry. I knew getting angry wasn't going to help, but I also knew I was beginning to lose control. 'So much for customer care,' I thought.

I waited for a gap between customers in the checkout next to me and asked the assistant what was happening. Without looking at me, they said the supervisor was trying to sort things out.

I would have liked to have asked what this meant, but by now I was feeling sick, my head was swimming and my breathing was getting tight. My palms were sweating, and I could feel a panic attack coming on. But I also felt very angry and entitled to an explanation. I wondered whether I should tell the assistant I was autistic, and could we move this to a quieter space, but by then it was too late.

And then a quiet inner voice said, 'Take refuge.'

Without thinking, I focused my attention on the feel of the shopping cart handle in my hands and took a breath. My eyes rested on the cart and I felt as if I was in a protected space, with the cart supporting me physically, something to hold on to. I began a formal breathing meditation as the world around me became quieter and less intrusive. *Breathing in, I know I am breathing in, breathing out, I know I am breathing out.* I began to imagine a community of meditators all around the world meditating with me and sending me loving kindness and support. And then the Buddha was with me: calming, reassuring, relaxing and compassionate. My anxiety and anger melted away and I felt calm. I began to think that maybe the shop staff were having a bad day. Maybe nothing like this had ever happened before. And maybe I am just a little too scary when I try and assert myself. I decided to wait patiently and give them time to sort things out.

I smiled at the supervisor as she returned with a large box containing my chair saying that she had managed to fix the situation by bypassing the computer and reordering a single chair for me. The other would be delivered tomorrow on a separate order, the details of which would be emailed to me. She placed the large box into my shopping cart and I think she even smiled a little. I thanked her and left the store, concentrating on my breathing and enjoying the moment. The sunshine, the blue sky and the breeze. People carrying their purchases out to their cars and chatting and laughing together. I was happy. I had achieved two things: I had a chair, through the efforts of the store supervisor, and I had managed to work through my feelings and stay calm because of the skills I had learned through meditation practice and with the loving support of the Triple Jewel.

CHAPTER 7

The Practical Application of the Dharma in Everyday Life

DR PERNILLE DAMORE

As an autistic person I think I find the Dharma and living the Dharma life so much easier than, perhaps, neurotypical people do. This is because the Dharma is basically a user's manual to socialization, conversation and how to go about my day. All the things I struggle with as an autistic person are described in the Dharma. And to make it even more attractive for me as an autistic person I think the Dharma is logic, it makes sense and the texts are suffused with riddles, clues and references. It's a puzzle that needs to be solved, and for every insight I get, I have to apply it to my life in order to understand the next riddle. It's absolutely brilliant for an autistic person! All the aspects of the Dharma I see my neurotypical spiritual friends struggling with are no problem at all for me because it fits perfectly with my autistic perception of reality and my autistic way of life.

I started meditating when I was 13 years old. I am Aspergers, but when I was a child it wasn't even a diagnosis, and for years to come the majority of diagnoses would only be of boys. You know, the ones sitting in the corner solving equations. We are a whole generation of women now in our 30s, 40s and 50s that all have been late diagnosed. So, we have had full lives of masking, coping and trying to make our lives work in a world that doesn't quite fit. Feeling like a square peg in a round hole. Anyway, I started meditating when I was 13 and kept at it because meditation helped me so much. Autistic burnout and daily feelings of being overwhelmed are a part of my life as with any other person with autism. And I don't know how my life would have been shaped if I hadn't found time twice a day to seek solitude, and just sit and breathe in quietness.

The person who taught me how to meditate suggested that I read the Satipatthana Sutta, so I did. And I have to say that changed everything for me. Most people use meditation to become more aware and more present in the moment. Autistic people rarely need that because we already, with our senses in overdrive, are very much aware! We need the opposite. We need sense deprivation, and we need to learn how to take one thing at a time and not be overwhelmed by the constant bombardment of our senses and our perception.

So, one of the key aspects of Buddhism is 'one-pointed-ness' – focusing on one thing only. When I bring my focus into one-pointedness I am no longer affected by, and a victim of, my senses. As with most people with Aspergers my senses are in overdrive. I wear blue glasses, earplugs and have a special ointment that numbs my sense of smell. This is because when I am out, I am often overwhelmed by the layers of scent and sound, and reflections of light. And on top of that I notice everyone and everything. But my meditation practice helps me develop one-pointedness, so I am no longer in the turmoil of all my senses. Instead, I have a practice of focusing on one thing and letting the rest 'be'. It is obviously very draining to be in that state of awareness all the time, but my meditation practice makes it possible for me to live a life where the ups and downs of autism are more manageable.

In the Satipatthana Sutta the Buddha says, 'When you're

walking, you're walking, when you're sitting, you're sitting, when you're standing, you're standing, when you're eating, you're eating.' For most people that seems trivial, almost superfluous, and they get annoyed or lose interest in the repetition of the Sutta. It takes most people years to really dive into the meaning of the Sutta and begin to understand. But to me, as an autistic person, when I read it the first time, that practice was anything but trivial and it taught me so much. As an autistic person, when I'm walking, I am very much aware that I am also smelling, hearing, tasting, thinking, feeling and noticing – which is so draining and exhausting. So, when I read the Satipatthana Sutta for the first time, I felt like I was given a 'cheat sheet' to life. That all I needed to do was just follow the recommendations in the Sutta. Bring the recommendations in the Sutta into my meditation practice and then expand my meditation practice to include my life off the cushion. And that has completely shaped my life! I think that besides getting a diagnosis, reading the Sutta at that young an age was the best thing that could have happened to me. Most late-diagnosed autistic people look back at their lives and see how they never had a chance! We just do not fit. Society is shaped to fit neurotypical people and anyone who is either 'more' or 'less' than the normal standard just doesn't fit – and nothing in society is aimed to fit us. So, our lives are very often confusing and very chaotic. And we often feel detached and not a part of what is going on around us. It was the same for me, but the Dharma offered me a clear guidance to life that really made sense.

The foundation of Buddhism is the teaching of conditioned existence, and it is formulated in four bullet points called the Four Noble Truths. Isn't it great that a manual to life comes in bullet points? I am telling you: the Dharma is a clear-cut autistic teaching! Anyway, conditioned existence is just a fancy way of saying, 'Nothing happens without something to start it, and if I remove what has started it – whatever has happened, will stop happening.' Complete logic. Makes so much sense. It's like physics, chemistry or maths; if I add, something will happen, if I subtract, it will stop happening. We see that all around us all the time. So, the foundation of Buddhism just fits perfectly into my autistic perception of reality. If I am nice to you, you will be nice to me. If I stop being nice to you, you will stop being nice to me. In my 13-year-old mind, that was such clear and logical guidance.

Obviously, it's more complicated than that, but I didn't learn that until much later in life. Now, back to conditioned existence and the Four Noble Truths. The first three truths are all about the fact that we get sick, we get old and we are going to die – and we really don't like that! We do everything we can to avoid being aware of that, and we spend so much effort and energy trying to divert our attention from that awareness. But the way we divert our attention actually gives us more suffering and dissatisfaction in life than the original problem ever could. The last of the four truths are eight clear guidelines (called the Noble Eightfold Path) on how we need to think, speak and behave and where we need to put value in order for us to be OK with everything horrible in life. This is obviously important on a big scale, but more important on a small scale in our day-to-day life. I would like to share how I use the eight guidelines from the Noble Eightfold Path with you because if you are an autistic person this might be as helpful to you as it has been to me.

The first guideline from the Noble Eightfold Path is 'Right View'. Applying 'Right View' into my life is creating a foundation for all decisions to be on a very high level of ethics. So, in general it's about me doing things mainly for the greater good rather than for selfish reasons. In general, that is super easy for autistic people because we tend to live by very clear rules of 'right or wrong' anyway. In general, autistic people don't lie, steal or cheat. We wouldn't break the law and we are good at putting ourselves aside if the outcome will be more beneficial for others. So, the first guideline is basically for me just to be my autistic self and do the right thing.

Let me give you an example. I am Danish but I am living alone in the UK. During the pandemic lockdowns I have not been able to visit my family and adult son and daughter-in-law in Denmark. All big events we have had in my family for the last year and a half I have not been able to be a part of in person and have had to participate via video call. Then came Christmas. I was so depressed and sad after almost a year in physical solitude and had really been looking forward to going home for Christmas. But when it came to it, I decided not to go. Not because I didn't want to go, but because it wouldn't have been ethically right for me to cross borders and fly from England to Germany and then on to Denmark during a pandemic! The UK government had the opinion that we could 'do what felt right' and most people took that as a green light to go and travel far for Christmas and to be with loved ones. Emotionally I was no different than the rest of the UK. I really wanted to travel home and smell, hug and be with my son and my family but ethically that wouldn't have been the right thing to do. So, I stayed here. So, to me 'Right View' is doing the right thing for the greater good and not being blinded or seduced by my emotional whims.

The second guideline from the Noble Eightfold Path is 'Right Thoughts', which obviously can be super difficult. But because it makes sense to me, I can easily practise this. In general, by 'doing the right thing', and focusing on doing the right thing, my thoughts will be affected. I will have a tendency to automatically get the 'Right Thoughts' by living with the 'Right View' as they are linked. But, as we all know, our ego is cunning and loves drama and problems. So, this is where meditation really helps me to clear my thoughts in order that they become 'right'. I use meditation to put my thoughts into perspective. Whenever I have a tendency to blame, shame and complain about a situation or other people, going into my room and sitting in silence quickly deflates the annoyance, aggravation and dissatisfaction I might be perceiving in my mind, body and feelings. So, on a practical level, what I do is simply sit down, close my eyes and be quiet. Very quickly my mind will pick up a topic and try to run with it. When that happens, I take my attention back from the thought 'out there' and back to me sitting here, just breathing and being. Doing nothing.

The most important thing when I do this is to bring the mind back without any fight. So, when I become aware that my mind is running off, I am not disappointed, or I don't want my mind to be different than it is. It's OK that it runs off because that is what the mind does. Just like the nose smells, the ears hear and the eyes see without me wanting them to do that, the mind thinks. So, the mind is not doing anything wrong. It's just doing what it's supposed to do. But I can choose to either focus on what the mind does and give it more attention and power, or I can choose to let it be and just bring my awareness away from the mind and into me just sitting here, being.

So, I bring my awareness back to no-thing-ness. Back to me just sitting here, quietly, with my eyes closed. That is a type of meditation called 'Just Sitting Meditation' and it is really a favourite of mine because it's very efficient but super demanding! Which is great. I like that. Just Sitting Meditation gives me something to master. And honestly, if I could pick only one special interest to truly master, I would choose to master my mind.

Another meditation that is super useful for developing 'Right Thoughts' is the Metta Bhavana. It's a traditional Buddhist meditation that evokes feelings of loving kindness. I set aside a specific amount of time and divide it into five intervals. So, it could be 25 minutes with five-minute intervals or 40 minutes with eight-minute intervals.

First, I start to think kind thoughts and send love and appreciation towards myself. Sending kind thoughts to my bodily functions, to my personality, to my choice of words, to everything that I perceive as me. That is the first interval of the meditation.

In the second interval of the meditation, I think kind thoughts and send love and appreciation towards someone I love and care about. I really appreciate their person, imagine I am hugging them, imagine them smiling and being happy and healthy. So, I am spending all the time in the second interval becoming really happy and content with them being in my life and wishing them happiness, joy and good health.

In the third interval, I think kind thoughts and send love and appreciation towards someone I don't know. It could be the manufacturer of my bed or the designer of my blender or the farmer who made the food I am going to have later today. But most times I pick a person I have noticed on the street during the day that I thought looked sad or stressed. You know, a person I noticed that really looked like they needed a hug. Then I recall them as they looked there in the street and bring them into my awareness. I give them my full attention and, just like I appreciated and thought kindly towards the person I love and care for, I do the same towards the person that I don't know and will never meet again – but who clearly needed someone to be kind to them. I am, in that moment, that someone.

The fourth interval is demanding, because I pick someone I have an issue with: someone I am angry at or annoyed by, or someone who I know doesn't like me. So, I bring that person into mind, think kindly of them and send love and appreciation towards them. For me it's rarely about people I don't like because I tend to like everyone and can very easily see other

people's points of view. So, for me, in this stage of the meditation, I usually think of someone that I like and appreciate but
who really doesn't like me! I find that useful because it helps
me get over myself and it helps me see the situation from their
angle. It puts a spotlight on whatever blaming, shaming or complaining is going on in my life towards the other person. But
maybe more importantly, it allows the other person to not like
me. I set them free to dislike me! I release all hooks and needs
I have to wanting them to see me in a different light. I set them
free to find me appalling, annoying, obnoxious or whatever else
they might think of me.

In the last and fifth interval of the meditation, I think kind
thoughts and send love and appreciation towards all of us. Not
only humans but towards every living being that I can think
of. Humans, animals, insects, all of us. I bring my awareness
towards people I know, people I have yet to meet and people I
will never meet. All of us. Every single being I am sharing the
earth with right now. And that is how I do the Metta Bhavana.
To me the Metta Bhavana is really good to put my life and the
way I see things into a proper perspective and it really helps me
developing 'Right Thoughts'.

The third guideline from the Noble Eightfold Path is 'Right
Speech' – which again (in general) is very easy for autistic people. We tend to speak the truth, not lie and rarely engage in
chit-chat and small talk. But what I have needed to be aware
of is that 'honesty without compassion is brutality'. Because I
am autistic, I always speak the truth – but being brutally honest
is in no one's interest. As well as relying on the speech precept
about harmonious speech, I also follow the advice the Buddha
gives. He says that I need to make sure that what I am going
to say is truthful, helpful and timely. If not, I serve the world
better by not commenting at all!

The fourth guideline from the Noble Eightfold Path is

'Right Action'. It is actually connecting to what I have just referred to. A good deed, no matter how kind, is unwanted if it is not given at the right time. It might be super kind of me to bring you a glass of water, but if you are not thirsty it's more of an empty gesture – or maybe even an inconvenience. So 'Right Action' is about me doing the right thing at the right time. It requires me to pay attention and see what support is *needed* in a situation, instead of focusing on me and letting my ego decide what support I *want* to provide.

The fifth guideline from the Noble Eightfold Path is 'Right Lifestyle'. This is where the guidelines change – the first four very much affect me internally, while the next four are a natural follow-on. So, if I have the right ethics, thought, speech and action, my lifestyle will automatically adapt and be a reflection of me. For example, regarding Right Lifestyle, if I have a foun-dational drive based on my ethics of loving kindness, I wouldn't choose to become a butcher or a soldier. Those two are obvious. I can't wish for all beings to be happy and healthy and then go out and kill them! So, it's important for me to be aware of my lifestyle on the more subtle scale. I wouldn't choose to become a journalist on *The Sun* or any other form of media that is not using its platform for loving kindness and compassion.

Most forms of media go to great lengths to divide and stir up negative emotions in their readers and viewers. So, part of my 'Right Lifestyle' is also not to read or indulge in that type of media. I become part of the problem, and not part of the solution, if I choose the kind of media that is not in line with my ethics. So, for my lifestyle to reflect my ethics, I need to make everything in my life – from my choice of job to how I choose to spend my days – in alignment with something that supports and helps humanity. Jobwise, I have chosen to become a naturopathic doctor and therapist and have spent the last 20+ years teaching people how to cure their chronic diseases and use meditation and mindfulness to ease their struggles and sufferings. I have written three books about this, and for the last 13 years I have been running online courses with weekly meditations and teachings. For me to have a 'Right Lifestyle' it is important that I 'walk the talk' and that I live my ethics in all aspects of my life.

The sixth guideline from the Noble Eightfold Path is the one I struggle with the most! No doubt about that! It's called 'Right Effort'. It is about not doing more or less than is needed in a situation – just doing the exact, right amount. I really struggle with that. I have a tendency to overdo my effort. I have this foundational drive in me that says, 'If I can do it, I should do it.' And that is far from the truth and rarely beneficial for me and the people around me! So, it's one I have been struggling with my entire life. As an Aspergers individual I tend to get very focused on a topic. Like Buddhism or biochemistry. Those are my special interests. And I build this 'Wikipedia-sized' knowledge base on the topic. That rarely happens with 'Right Effort'! But I also struggle with 'Right Effort' if there is something I don't understand. For me to experience mental calm I need to understand things. I really struggle leaving a topic 'half-sorted'. I will go to great lengths to seek information that will clarify things so I will understand, and *then* I can relax or meditate. Because I know this to be an issue of mine, I am practising letting go. To let things be as they are. To accept reality as it is and try not to change what is needed right now – just let go of my need to change it. To help me with this guideline I rely on the precept that promotes 'stillness, simplicity and contentment'.

Let me give you an example. This summer I have been struggling a lot with my health. The situation has not been improved by me feeling isolated and alone. I am a part of an allotment space that I share with two of my spiritual friends from my sangha. But because I have been struggling, I haven't had the surplus energy to go there and socialize. They are two lovely women and I really enjoy their company, but when I am in 'autistic overwhelm' everything is just too much. Now, a part of me really doesn't want to accept reality as it is and that part of me wants to 'pull myself together' and just 'go there'. However, 'Right Effort' is about not doing too much and not doing too little. It's about finding the right amount of involvement in the 'middle way'. I use the precept of 'stillness, simplicity and contentment' by bringing my focus to what I am content with right now. What I have, right now, in my life, that I am content with, that doesn't need to change because I am content as it is. And then I focus on that. So, I bring my attention from wanting more than I have (to go to the allotment) or from wanting 'other' than I have (the surplus and health to socialize) to what I actually have right now that I am content with.

The seventh guideline from the Noble Eightfold Path is 'Right Focus' and that is what I have just been talking about. This is when I focus on what is beneficial instead of what I want. My 'Right Focus' is always in my awareness of 'just being' rather than what my ego wants.

The eighth guideline from the Noble Eightfold Path is 'Right Mindfulness' and it's the culmination of the previous seven guidelines. It's where I harvest of all my efforts and it's where my entire life of living the Dharma comes to fruition. To me, it's also where my autistic personality and my autistic perception of reality become woven into the Dharma and that brings us right back to me as a 13-year-old starting to meditate and reading the Satipatthana Sutta – the discourse on mindfulness.

So, to finish. If you too are an autistic person, I hope I have been helpful in making you see how much the Dharma has to offer. But also, how easy the Dharma actually is for you because you are autistic and many of our autistic traits fit perfectly into the teachings.

If you are not autistic but you are practising the Dharma as a teacher, centre director or practice group leader, then I also hope I have been helpful in bringing to light how this autistic person applies the Dharma to her life – and maybe I have even made you see the Dharma with autistic eyes! I wish you and yours, health and happiness.

CHAPTER 8

Loving Kindness

How Meditating Helps Me Feel Better about Myself

ISH TANNAHILL

I am 25 years old and discovered Buddhism when I was 18 years old. I was initially with the Triratna Buddhist Community, but I moved away from this sangha for personal reasons. I joined a Community of Interbeing sangha a couple of years ago but have been unable to attend the main meetings as I struggle to meditate for long periods because it can cause me distress. I am also not very good at handling group situations. Along with my autism, I have mental health and physical health problems, which I am now getting the right help for. I am also an active member in the LGBTQ+ community and I am part of an online Rainbow sangha. I am beginning to study and will be looking at starting a degree soon.

My mother used to read stories about meditation and Buddhism to me when I was a child. She is not Buddhist herself but has an interest in meditation and Buddhism. This inspired me as a young adult to attend the local Buddhist centre. I went in boldly exclaiming, 'I would like to book on a retreat.' I really wanted to explore the teachings in depth. There happened to be a young person on the desk who introduced me to the under-35s night that took place every week. He suggested I join for a few months and attend the retreat at the end of the year as well. From then on, I was a regular attender. I found the teachings and meditations fitted very well with what I believed in and I was constantly learning.

Having autism did mean it took time for me to take in all the information as I struggle to process things as quickly as neurotypical people. I pored over texts and teachings and tried to understand them as best I could. I wasn't yet confident enough to ask for help in this. I also find silent, single-focus meditation very difficult to sit through for long periods. This is because I can get very cyclical in my thoughts, which causes me distress. A very good friend from the centre offered to help me and sent me recordings of shorter, guided meditations. To this day I still use them regularly. They have helped me to deepen my practice and build a better connection with myself and others. Here is a short, guided meditation on loving kindness you might like to try:

Get yourself into a comfortable position and take a few deep breaths. Allow your eyes to close. Become aware of the space you are in, and your body, in this environment.

Now bring to mind a good friend. This may be a family member, friend or even your pet.

Take a moment to visualize them as if they were sitting in front of you. Imagine what they sound like and what their laugh is like.

Now begin to send them well wishes. If it helps, repeat in your head: 'May they be well; may they be happy.'

Focus in on your heart area and think of the love radiating from that area as you continue to think of your friend. Just like you, they have struggles and low points, but continue to send loving kindness and know that you are contributing to their wellbeing.

Now bring those warm wishes to yourself. Repeat: 'May I be well; may I be happy.'

Send yourself love and kindness. Focus in on your heart area and feel the love radiating from this point.

Continue for a moment to send well wishes to yourself and allow yourself permission to receive them.

Repeat: 'May I accept myself and love myself,' and really focus in on yourself and allowing yourself permission to receive this loving kindness.

In the final stage, begin to focus on everyone in your neighbourhood. Send them well wishes repeating: 'May they be well; may they be happy.'

May everyone you meet today receive this loving kindness.

Feel your heart radiate and reach out to all these beings.

Now set the intention to be kind and loving to yourself throughout the day. Take a few deep breaths, focus back in on your body. Begin to wiggle your fingers and toes and open your eyes bringing yourself back into the room.

Following this guided meditation on loving kindness helps me to feel better about myself and other people. It also stops me getting upset, which is what would happen if I were to sit in silent meditation.

Unfortunately, because I battle mental health challenges, I have ended up in hospital several times. This has made practising very difficult. Once I nervously asked the Chaplaincy at the hospital if there was help I could have with my practice. He replied, 'We actually have a Buddhist volunteer who I can get in touch with for you!' I was so relieved and excited to begin a fresh start with the Dharma.

The Buddhist Chaplaincy volunteer visited me regularly on the ward. She went through short meditations that really seemed to click, and we slowly went through teachings, practised rituals and recited sutras. The Buddha's 'Discourse on Love' was my favourite part.

He or she who wants to attain peace should practice being upright, humble, and capable of using loving speech. He or she will know how to live simply and happily, with senses calmed, without being covetous and carried away by the emotions of the majority. Let him or her not do anything that will be disapproved of by the wise ones.

(And this is what he or she contemplates:)

May everyone be happy and safe, and may all hearts be filled with joy.

May all beings live in security and in peace—beings who are frail or strong, tall or short, big or small, invisible or visible, near or far away, already born, or yet to be born. May all of them dwell in perfect tranquillity.

Let no one do harm to anyone. Let no one put the life of anyone in danger. Let no one, out of anger or ill will, wish anyone any harm.

Just as a mother loves and protects her only child at the risk of her own life, cultivate boundless love to offer to all living beings in the entire cosmos. Let our boundless love pervade the whole universe, above, below, and across. Our love will know no obstacles. Our heart will be absolutely free from hatred and enmity. Whether standing or walking, sitting or lying, as long as we are awake, we should maintain this mindfulness of love in our own heart. This is the noblest way of living.

Free from wrong views, greed, and sensual desires, living in beauty and realizing Perfect Understanding, those who practice boundless love will certainly transcend birth and death. (Metta Sutta, Sutta Nipata 1.8; Thich Nhat Hanh, 2021)

Reading through this sutra with the Buddhist Chaplaincy volunteer, and discussing its relevance to my life, helped me to feel good about myself. Eventually, I found that I deepened my practice in the meditations. I developed a connection with my body. My autism prevents me from really getting any physical cues with my body, so body scan meditations and following the breath were revelations to me. You can find examples of both of these forms of meditation by searching online. It's taken time to get there but I am a lot more aware of my physical self and how that can relate and interweave with my mind.

I have also found the practice of impermanence incredibly useful to me – nothing is permanent, and things are always changing. I struggle with change, and I set myself rigid routines. The idea of impermanence has allowed me to loosen these barriers and accept reality for what it truly is, ever changing. Although times have been tough, I would not look back from the Dharma. I've found it fits with my beliefs and values and it also helps me to manage my autism and find the good things about being autistic as well. I still regularly meet up online with my friend, the Buddhist Chaplaincy volunteer, and we discuss the Dharma.

CHAPTER 9

The Five Mindfulness Trainings and How They Help Me to Be Authentically Autistic

DR LIAN BEIJERS (*Courageous Connection of the Heart*)

Out of all the spiritual traditions I have encountered in my life, I have always felt most attracted to Buddhism. And yet, I did not really get into it until I was well into my 20s, because even though the majority of what I knew about Buddhism seemed very logical, there were a number of things I found terribly frustrating about the teachings. For example, I felt that the concept of non-self was diametrically opposed to the concept of reincarnation, and I could not help but get a little bit angry at the concept of karma as some kind of cosmic retribution. All of that changed when I encountered someone who introduced me to the Plum Village tradition and the teachings of Thich Nhat Hanh – who is often referred to as Thay, the Vietnamese word for teacher. His books and talks showed me ways to interpret these concepts that were different from the definitions I had learned from popular culture, and as I learned more, my feelings of dissonance were slowly replaced with a sense of relief and homecoming.

It did not take long for me to join my first sangha meeting, and I was hooked immediately. After only three or four months of practice, I got the opportunity to join a Plum Village-style retreat for young people from all over the Netherlands. There were a few social challenges at the beginning, but I felt very much at home there, because the acceptance I experienced from the group was beyond what I had ever experienced before. At this retreat I was introduced to Buddhist ethics in the form of the Five Mindfulness Trainings (see Appendix II). These are a modern version of the five precepts developed, during the time of the Buddha, as a foundation for the practice of the entire lay community. The first training is to protect life and to decrease violence in oneself, the family and society. The second training is to practise social justice and generosity as well as not stealing and not exploiting other living beings. The third is the practice of responsible sexual behaviour in order to protect individuals, couples, families and children. The fourth is the practice of deep listening and loving speech to restore communication and to reconcile. The fifth is about mindful consumption and helps us not bring toxins and poisons into our body or mind.

I decided to commit to practising these Trainings, because there was something about them that just felt right. Before my introduction to the Five Mindfulness Trainings, my life looked pretty much like that of the average neurotypical even though I am autistic. I had a decent social life, and I would regularly go to parties or the cinema with my friends. After work I watched a lot of Netflix, and I enjoyed gaming, listening to music and reading lots of fantasy books. However, after my retreat I started questioning why I was doing all of these things, and what their effects were on me. I noticed that I was often trying to escape from my uncomfortable feelings of tiredness, stress or overstimulation by consuming things like Netflix or the news. And this would generally just leave me more restless than before – which was leading me to consume even more. I was also doing many things just because my neurotypical peers were doing them, and I didn't want to be left out when people were discussing certain books or going to the next Marvel movie together. I was already vegan before I encountered the practice, but I was still drinking alcohol occasionally, although the social pressure to drink started bothering me more and more.

Because I am so sensitive to the things I consume, whether it is food or some form of entertainment, the Training about mindful consumption was a natural first focus for me. Within the space of a few months, I dropped many of my old habits. Now, I no longer go to the cinema, I hardly ever watch TV anymore, I only play tabletop games and the only books I read nowadays are about work stuff or about the practice. I also stopped drinking alcohol completely, which made it much easier to say no when someone would offer me an alcoholic beverage.

As time went on, the other Trainings started to become more influential as well. For example, I started to realize that I did not really enjoy the online dating I was engaging in, and that it was OK to want a loving relationship based on compassion and connection, where sex is not the most important factor. My dedication to protecting life also increased – I stopped killing bugs of any kind, and I got more involved in environmental activism.

In Plum Village, there is a lot of emphasis on the fact that the Five Mindfulness Trainings are not meant to be some kind of strict standard that we need to measure up to in order to be a good practitioner. They are a concrete expression of the Four Noble Truths and the Noble Eightfold Path. As such, they are meant to help relieve our suffering and bring us greater freedom, insight and happiness, and we are encouraged to experiment and try for ourselves if they do. Personally, I do not feel limited by the Trainings at all. On the contrary, it feels like the Five Mindfulness Trainings give me permission to finally shape my life in a way that is more in line with my needs as an autistic person. The Trainings help me see all of the ways in which modern-day society is not compatible with my nervous system, and they make it easier for me to express my core values of love and compassion in the way I conduct my day-to-day life. I have fewer meltdowns because I am more aware of the consequences of my consumption patterns, and I think that, all in all, my life feels more authentic now.

I have also noticed that my autism makes it easier for me to follow the Trainings to some extent. On average, it seems that neurotypical people tend to struggle more with certain elements of the Trainings. For example, it seems harder for them to commit to a vegan diet, or to let go of things like drinking alcohol or social media, even when they think it's a good idea to do so. I think that because I am more sensitive to the effects of these types of consumption, the connection is more obvious and the negative effects are more severe, which makes it easier to quit doing something. I also think that making decisions and sticking to them is more achievable for me because I tend to easily experience strong cognitive dissonance. So, once I decide something is the better option, I usually just keep doing that.

There are other parts of the practice that do not come as easily for me. For example, I find the training on loving speech pretty challenging sometimes. Because of my autism, I have never been good at lying. Instead, I tend to be brutally honest. However, since I have encountered the practice, I have learned that it is important not just to speak the truth, but to do so in a tactful way, and that can be challenging. I like to think I am fairly good at non-violent communication, but I am noticing that that becomes more difficult when I get more tense or upset. I have a strong habit of complaining, even ranting a little bit, when I get frustrated.

Practising within the sangha really helps to grow my under-standing of my own challenges and the practice of the Five Mindfulness Trainings. I find it very inspiring to hear other sangha friends share about their interpretation of the Trainings, because I always learn something new or gain a different per-spective. Over the past year, I have come to understand that not all changes need to happen right away, and that not everything is a yes-or-no decision. In Plum Village, Buddhist practice is often described as a kind of gardening. The Five Mindfulness Trainings are compared to seeds that are planted in the garden of our consciousness, and with careful tending, these seeds will grow into something beautiful. It is only a figure of speech, but it describes how I have come to experience my practice very well.

I have become more patient – trying to be perfect just stresses me out, so I have stopped trying. For example, I did not attempt to stop complaining altogether immediately, because I knew I would not be able to do that. Instead, I tried to observe what was happening in moments where I felt the need to express myself in this way. I wanted to pay attention to how my behaviour affects my family and friends, without judging myself for not being able to quit. After a few weeks of practising in this way, I developed some capacity to stop myself, either after a few minutes or even before I got started. I feel very encouraged by this development, and I have faith that if I continue to practise in this way, I will eventually be able to transform this habit energy in me even more.

I feel like the Five Mindfulness Trainings give me permission to stop participating in the parts of our society that are not so well suited for my nervous system. And that my autism conveys a sizable advantage when it comes to following them. Over time, I have developed trust that if I stay committed to practising the Trainings in ways that suit me, I will continue to grow as a per-son, developing more freedom, insight and happiness.

CHAPTER 10

Buddhism and Parenting

How Mindfulness of the Breath Helps
Me Listen to My Autistic Daughter

LUCY LIU

My daughter was diagnosed with autism in 2005 when she was three-and-a-half years old. She also has language processing, emotional regulation (particularly with anxiety) and social communication difficulties. She often experiences a fight-or-flight reaction and a frozen mental state. Her mind ruminates a lot on past stressful memories, and she can become very emotional. She often relives past experiences which have caused a lot of anxiety.

The other challenge my daughter faces is that she obsesses with music and online videos. It is hard to shift her attention to something else. Any disagreement about this, or moving her from one thing to another, can cause her to get emotional and her body shakes. When this happens, I become aware of my anxiety and my body tenses up. I used to suppress my emotions but have gradually learned to care for my feelings and regulate my emotions. Meditating on slowing the breath calms my heart and my emotions. My body softens and I can let go of stressful emotions and body tension. This helps me to create a peaceful place for my child in her home environment. I find meditating on the breath interesting, and I am able to sense universal love and a connection with others. This comes easily through developing awareness of my breath in my daily living. This awareness inspires me to continue to practise.

I feel that my life has become very stressful and anxiety provoking bringing up a child with autism. There are endless mental and physical demands from my daughter's needs on a day-to-day basis. I also have to attend health, social care and educational meetings and deal with all of that stress. I was curious when I heard that mindfulness meditation could help me and improve my wellbeing. So, this led me, in 2006, to try it at the Compassion Centre near where I live. I also visited a Zen Buddhist centre in Hexham and a spiritual community, Samye Ling, in Scotland. It was at Samye Ling that I first looked at Thich Nhat Hanh's books related to Buddhist practice. I felt this was simple and easier to implement than other traditional Buddhism I was familiar with. So, I joined a Plum Village sangha practice group in the north-east of England.

When I first started to practise mindfulness, I noticed that my mind was very busy in the past and future, and so was limited. There were often a lot of memories that continued to impact my emotions and body in my daily life. They could be images or voices appearing in my head and I could be stuck for a few hours without having noticed this was happening. Gradually, by being mindful, I learned to allow them to talk to me and I patiently listened to what they were saying without judgement. Then I would gently bring my attention to my breathing to soften my body. Sometimes I used my hands to touch my heart or touch my painful body to comfort it to let my emotions out. This is a meditation (one that I have adapted from a Plum Village meditation) that I recite to myself while I am following my breath:

Breathing in, I know I am breathing in
Breathing out, I know I am breathing out
Breathing in, I know I am breathing deeply
Breathing out, I know I am breathing slowly
Breathing in, I know I am calming my body
Breathing out, I know I am relaxing
Breathing in, I know I am smiling
Breathing out, I know I am letting go
Breathing in, I know that this is the present moment
Breathing out, I know that this is a wonderful moment

These days, I also use other mindful practices in my daily life when I am moving my body, listening to music and songs, eating, drinking, cooking and walking. This helps me to connect with myself and move to calm and peaceful feelings. My mind can then stop judging my daughter (and the professionals involved in her care and education). I can listen to what my daughter is telling me and I am more able to think how I can help her in a practical way. Most of the time, I need to make 'reasonable adjustments' to help her to reduce her anxiety. For example: provide written instructions for her; break down tasks into small steps (with pictures and visual images); and slow her down so that she can do things one step at a time. Then we can connect with each other really well and do things together. Things like walking together in the fresh air. My favourite way of walking is to be aware of my feet on the earth and, with a slow pace, walk step by step. Buddhists call this 'walking meditation'. We combine this with looking around us – watching the sky and the trees – and noticing our feelings as we are breathing.

My daughter and I also like to prepare food and eat together – our favourite is Chinese dumplings. We like to use sweet potato noodles, vegetables, wild garlic, tofu, sesame oil and soya sauce. And we drink different herbal teas like ginger, lemon and honey. Bubble tea from China Town is a particular favourite of ours.

We enjoy doing movement to music together with body movements like tree shaking and 'body cross movement', which helps with balance. We also do yoga with 'face and head tapping', which helps to reduce facial tension. I notice that if we can calm down and do activities like these together, she will have less mental stress and sleep better. I have to be careful though. Because of her autism, she can't face too much talking or too much of me demanding that we walk or do activities together. I normally use simple language to engage with her, most of the time encouraging her to enjoy walking outdoors to ease her body tension and be aware of her feelings. Then I shift our attention to nature by breathing and sensing our feelings as we watch the sky and enjoy the trees. When she sings songs, I normally move my body to the music and we try to enjoy ourselves together in the moment.

I have to remind myself that Buddhist teachings can over-load people with autism. There can be too much written and verbal information and this can particularly overload autistic people who have language processing difficulties. This is a shame because our common humanity should mean that Bud-dhism is for everyone. Buddhism reveals human suffering – from thoughts and feelings about being judged to difficulties with ego and attachment. Mindfulness is about developing an awareness of the truth. It is about wisdom, self-compassion and practising and learning through our own experiences. First, we learn to be curious, then we accept how we think and feel, and then we go on to learn to soften – which enables us to be gentle with ourselves and others. Only then can we truly connect with other people. But groups and friendships can overwhelm my daughter – and Buddhist theory is too complicated to grasp. She 'walks away from it'. I would really like to find a way of helping her that doesn't overwhelm her – maybe a five-minute online group meditation with other autistic young people who also get easily overwhelmed by it all.

I only wish that my daughter could learn these things through being able to learn about Buddhism and develop her own practices. But the way things are, she doesn't want to know – saying that it is all too much for her. The Dharma is too complicated and meditations go on for too long. I am always looking for ways to introduce her to Buddhism by making things simple and not overload her.

But Buddhism has helped me a lot and in turn I am able to help my daughter. I used to engage a lot with past memories and most of the time I felt trapped in my emotional world. I noticed that when I became emotionally triggered by past unpleasant memories, I often sensed a blockage of my throat as well. But to help with this experience I have learned to gently bring my attention to my feet, to walk softly and slowly, and to consciously connect my breath to my abdomen and chest to make sure I get fresh air in my lungs. By doing this, I can get a sense of the love and kindness of the earth and air. This helps to ease my emotions and soften my body. My mind can also become fresh and creative after doing this kind of meditation. I feel it is gradually helping me to stay calm. Nowadays, I set an alarm to remind myself to pause, slow down and go out for a walk. If I have a busy day, it's good to get some fresh air. I also notice that I can apply meditation techniques in any situation – such as at home or attending meetings. Mindfulness helps my body move from a stressed and anxious state to one of calmness. I find I can concentrate on and listen to other people better, but most especially, listen to my daughter.

CHAPTER 11

My Classroom Is My Sangha

Compassion and Loving Kindness in Special Needs Education

DENA RASHKOVER (*Piyadithha*)

My children are my wise teachers and my noble friends. I have been a teacher of special needs children for 28 years in a public elementary school 'separate classroom' setting in North Carolina (NC).[1] Some of the children I work with are autistic and some have sensory impairments. Most are considered to have moderate to severe cognitive deficits. They present with multiple handicaps and have varying language abilities from non-verbal, deaf (and learning sign language) to highly verbal. Essentially, we are a hodgepodge melting pot of diagnoses, abilities, and souls. Most of the kids I teach are with me for six years and there are usually from six to ten children at any one time with me and my assistant. Working with these children is my calling and my passion. It is my practice. Every day I am inspired by these wise souls. Every day I am in awe. Every day I learn something about life and myself – and I get drawn back to what really matters to me the most.

I believe my teaching reinforces my practice as a Bodhisattva.

---

[1] The language I use to describe my students in this account reflects current NC State terminology.

My engagement with my students is so deeply tied to it. I have always been one that would self-define as spiritual, but not religious. I am not into dogma or established rituals, but more of a free, earthy spirit. That is true for both my personal and professional life. Twenty-five years into my teaching career, at the age of 47, I took the step to become a student in a formal 'sangha setting'. I was introduced through a mindfulness class at my local sangha, Heartwood Refuge in Western NC. It changed my life, it gave me a tribe of adults to call community, and it is my spiritual home along with my classroom. Before that, I was a lone wolf, deeply connected to a spiritual calling, and firmly rooted in love and compassion. My style of teaching and personality have never seemed to quite blend in with the norm. My whole personality does not really line up with the norm. I have felt misunderstood and like an outcast for most of my life – childhood through adulthood. I am short (4'9"), kind of hyper, and can be outspoken. For years, I fought that. Then I realized it is a gift. My kids need someone like me to help them on their path and to be their advocate. They also do not quite fit in, and not everyone accepts and sees them as the perfect beings they are. I call us the land of the 'misfit toys' and myself the tribal leader. I see my kids as innate Buddhas. I am both teacher and student. It is a rich, deep dive into so many aspects of what Buddhism is rooted in. I think it is quite auspicious that my room number is 101. I love that; it is fitting and perfect.

I am lucky to have always had a school community and families that are open minded. I work hard to create an open-door policy, so my kids have the experience of being part of a greater community, and it has resulted in many unexpected opportunities for everyone involved. We have 'yoga buddy Friday', which has resulted in so many new social and learning opportunities for both classes. My friend teaches 2nd grade and each Friday her class comes in for a 30-minute session with us.

It was always special to see her class engage and encourage my kids to participate to the best of their abilities. Some of my kids were literally more flexible than the mainstream kids! In the lunchroom each class is assigned to a separate table. However, because I have so few kids in my room, there is always empty space. Every day, unasked and unsolicited, kids from other rooms come sit with my kids and visit with them. Our local high school has a program called Occupational Course of Study (OCS). It is a class that teaches work-based life skills training for high-functioning special-needs adolescents. I have interns from the local high school who spend a semester learning job skills that can lead them to a career in day care or working in day programs for persons with disabilities. In these ways, I keep the door to my classroom open for the benefit of my children, and others as well.

From a broader community perspective, I connect with my local farmers, musicians, and our school resource officers. All of them volunteer time and talent in my room. We get concerts, visits, food (for me to distribute to families), and offers for amazing field trips. We love to go out and about, and library story hour followed by lunch and frozen yogurt is our favorite community outing. All these activities are designed to build community – bringing people to my kids and bringing my kids to a larger community.

I have a real passion for kids with behavioral problems who are in the mainstream setting. My room is a magnet for kids in regular classes who are often aggressive, are non-compliant, and display significant challenges in their class setting. I pair up with the regular education teachers and provide mentorship for kids who need a place away to calm down, a safe space, and a reason to even come to school. It is a real demonstration of community. I cannot tell you how often those 'challenging' kids are the best peer mentors, especially the most significant and aggressive males. They come to my room and just connect with the kids in such a special way.

So, how do I bring the Dharma and practice to my kids? I do not think I even bring it; I believe it is already there. The entire nature of the dynamic energy-flow and synchronicity between myself and the kids makes it easy. My job is to bring out and nurture what they already come in with. They bring it to me, and to each other, as much as I bring it to them. It is such a beautiful experience. The community we bring together both within our school and beyond makes room 101 like a little Dharma center! Instead of being the 'outcasts', we are the most 'popular' class in the school. That does not always happen with special needs populations.

How do Buddhism and the special education classroom co-exist? As odd as it may seem to people who do not truly understand the Dharma, or to people who can't see the true nature of these kids, it seems as if the two would be separate. But it is not like that at all. There are so many ways in which the Buddha's message is demonstrated in a real-world, pure, unadulterated way. It is beautiful in its essence and simplicity.

Let's look at the basics of Buddhism. First of all, the Four Noble Truths tell us about the nature of suffering, the root of suffering, the cessation of suffering, and the path out of suffering. The simple truth is that in life there is suffering. There are the 'biggies' like aging, death, and loss. There are also the little things that catch us off guard. For me they are graying hair, laugh lines, and the house not being enough in order. But my truest deepest suffering is rooted in fear and doubt. When I go down this road, my fears are rooted in being judged, being fired, and being abandoned. My history with my family has set me up for the fear of abandonment. Mine is an old pattern and story, told time and time again. But there is a sense of healing I get from my teaching experience. My kids don't judge me, unconditional love in its pure sense. I need that, and we all do. It is just rare that we find that kind of love between people. It certainly is one of the reasons I love teaching.

I had a student, Brody.[2] He and I were always very connected at a level that words cannot express. We were 'old souls' together. One day, he was just staring at me, not saying anything. I asked him if he was OK, and he said yes. He kept staring at me for what seemed like an unusually long time. Finally, I asked him why he was staring at me. (In the adult world, I was thinking, food in teeth, bad hair day, etc.) Brody looked right at me and said, 'Because you are beautiful Dena.' I cried. That was a hard day for me. I had to look deep into myself and let that sink in. We all deserve that kind of love, we all should be open to giving and sharing that, but it took me a long time to accept that I, too, am fully lovable.

When we see right into each other's true beauty and soul, there is no suffering. But looking deeper, what is the actual cause and root of the majority of my suffering? My own delusions, need for control, attachments, and aversions. That is basic 'Introduction to Buddhism 101'. In practice, we evaluate and work with the root of suffering and uproot it. I am sure most of us are aware of what the roots of our suffering are. As 'functional' adults, we create so much of our own needless drama and suffering that leads to a lifetime of trying to navigate our way out. We cling, we hold on, we judge, and we create a spiral of Samsara. But what would it really be like to skip out on the suffering and just live life as it is? Think about that. How much of my suffering and your suffering is self-created? Can you imagine life in a simpler form?

That question brings me back to the basics of Buddhism.

---

2   I have changed the names of the children in this account to protect their identities.

Let's take a look at 'present moment awareness'. Buddhism and the practice of mindfulness is all about being in the present moment. I spend time both during meditation and my daily engagements working on being in the 'now'. I can easily get caught up in planning the future or lost in thinking, 'What if?' I have worked hard to stop ruminating on a past that is gone and I cannot control. That has taken a tremendous amount of work and energy on my part and continues to be a work in progress. But I am now able to give a large part of my ability to stay in the moment to keeping the world as safe and calm as I can for my kids.

I work with kids who have been together day after day for years, and they are a family. Put that together with severe difficulties with understanding how to work through their emotions – they get into sibling spats, take each other's toys, and annoy each other. Like I said, family. But here is the beauty: it seems to me that the moment is over when it is over. They appear to move on. In my years, I have never seen a kid, as far as I can tell, hold on to a grudge or struggle to let go of a tiff. They knock over each other's block towers, take each other's toys, and even 'tell' on each other. I have learned the best thing I can do is stay out of it and let them figure it out. And they do. Every day seems to be a new beginning. The bus comes, drops them off, they spend the day together, ride the bus (or mom bus), and start over fresh. How awesome is that? They give the impression that the moment is over, move on, let it go. I struggle with that myself all the time. I can be so super critical of myself and shoot off a second arrow like a wild woman, but when I pause to reflect, I too am learning how to let things go. And my children set a wonderful example for me to follow.

As I observe my kids at school, I am amazed at how they seem to be completely engaged in the moment. There is a schedule we follow, which really helps them navigate the day.

I have established a comfortable, predictable routine that makes sense to them. I use picture cues to bring the abstract concept of time to the level of concrete understanding they require. When it is play time, we play; when it is recess, it is recess; when it is art time, we do art. I love the enthusiasm my kids bring to each activity. I work hard on planning hands-on fun stuff that is both relevant and challenges them. It keeps them so engaged. Most of the time it is messy, but messy is fun! Paint, glitter, free-form expression: serious fun! The true joy in being 100% into whatever is happening is what we aim for. How many of us are actually free enough from ourselves and our intellectual sides to experience that for more than brief instances? We have to spend lifetimes, go on retreat, and work on meditation techniques to get to that space. For them, it seems to be a natural state of being. I think that is Buddha nature.

Now, where are we with our look at basic Buddhism? Time to look at the practice of compassion and kindness. Mine is a classroom full of the most beautiful souls I have seen. The fact that they present with so many global needs is irrelevant. The children are significantly challenged cognitively but their innate wisdom is beyond measure. I have seen so many examples of giving without expectation and true understanding of compassion and care. I had a student, Sam, who was blind. He would often trip over toys or knock into chairs if they were in his path. It never frustrated him or upset him – he would just get up. Over time, the other kids in the room noticed and recognized what happened. Given even more time, the kids would see the objects in his path, stop playing, and push chairs in, move toys, and help Sam navigate the room safely. No one had to teach them that, they did not seek praise, they just somehow knew. Compassion and kindness without expectation of praise or gain.

Once, I had another student, Donna, who had experienced severe mental, physical, and sexual trauma at home. She was on the autism spectrum, was significantly cognitively challenged, had encephalopathy linked to arsenic poisoning, and was schizophrenic. Donna hallucinated and talked to herself daily. There were times in the room when she would just scream, masturbate in front of the class, and cry. She had friends in class though, friends who somehow understood her need for physical and emotional comfort. Donna would lay her head down on their lap and they would just stroke her hair until she calmed down. I think that is serious compassion and great wisdom. It is the Bodhisattva way and an example of the spirit and true balance of wisdom and compassion. I cannot teach that innate knowing, but I can encourage it and lead by example. It is inspirational to see compassion and kindness, in its purest and simplest form, played out daily in my classroom. The Buddha said, 'Noble friends and companions are the whole of holy life.' The connections that are built and foundational in my classroom demonstrate that. We take care of ourselves, each other, hold hands, and walk our path together. It is through kindness, joy, determination, and compassion in action. Called by any name, it is beautiful in its essence and simplicity. It is truly the Bodhisattva vow and way.

CHAPTER 12

Joining a Sangha

Finding a Way to Friendship

JANE GARRATT (*Prajnanandi*)

In 2018 I was ordained into the Triratna Buddhist Order – a spiritual community of people who have pledged themselves to following the Buddhist path to enlightenment. This was the culmination of ten years of effort and exploration, joyously completed. Something that had, at times, seemed impossible for me had finally happened! I want to take you on the journey of how I got to where I am now. It's the story of how I was able to move from the statement 'I don't have friends' to being able to say, 'I have many friends.' It's the story of how Buddhism helped me to develop rich, close, emotional connections with people who are not family members.

For most of my life I have had to work around the fact that I think differently from other people, without knowing why. It was obvious to me that I saw some things very clearly while others were a complete mystery to me. I can see patterns and how these patterns connect. It's clear that if you act in a certain way then certain results will usually follow. But I find it very hard to read non-verbal communication. Mostly I just don't see it, but when I do see it, I often misinterpret what I'm seeing.

If you say something to me, I hear your words but I don't pick up on the context behind the words.

As a child I was often ill and I was also very shy. As a result, I regularly missed school or was by myself at school. I got on perfectly well with people, but did not develop close friendships. I learned early on the importance of being part of a group for survival and found a group that was prepared to accept me. These girls were very tolerant and were happy for me to be part of the group at school. But they all met up outside school as well and I didn't join these outings. I was never invited to go with them and it never occurred to me to ask.

The same patterns were there when I left school. I worked well with people, I was intelligent and articulate, well organized and could explain things clearly – but I made no close friends. There were work relationships which I enjoyed, but they never developed into anything outside work. People asked me about problem solving or process issues but never about emotional problems or other personal difficulties. We sometimes went out as a work group but never simply for a coffee. The statement 'I have no friends' was accurate at this time. I did not miss having close friendships but sometimes wondered what it would be like to have these relationships. Other people seemed to enjoy them!

Then, when I was 50 years old, I met Buddhism. I wasn't looking for Buddhism at that point, I simply wanted to learn how to meditate. There were three possible Buddhist groups within my local area and I wrote to them all asking if they had chairs to sit on to meditate, because I find getting up from the ground challenging. Only one group replied, so I decided to go with them and went into the local Triratna Buddhist centre for the first time.

I'd never been anywhere like this centre. I was welcomed at the door. The place was full of people chatting in small groups, with lots of laughter. People invited me into the groups and said hello. We all went together into the shrine room and then after the meditation came out and chatted more – with a large array of teas and biscuits! I knew that there was something different and wonderful about the place and I wanted to be part of it. I wondered if, here, I could find people who would continue to talk to me. So, I started attending the centre regularly. The only real difficulty I had at this point was that people wanted to hug me and I didn't want to be hugged by people I didn't know well. It was very uncomfortable.

One of the distinctive focuses of Triratna Buddhism is the crucial importance of sangha, the spiritual community of people who follow the Buddha's teachings. Sangharakshita built the movement with this exchange between the Buddha and Ananda at its core:

Ananda said to the Blessed One, 'This is half of the holy life, lord: admirable friendship, admirable companionship, admirable camaraderie.'

'Don't say that, Ananda. Don't say that. Admirable friendship, admirable companionship, admirable camaraderie is actually the whole of the holy life. When a monk has admirable people as friends, companions, & comrades, he can be expected to develop & pursue the noble eightfold path.' (SN 45.2 'The whole of the holy life' – Access to Insight, 2013)

Triratna Buddhists work hard to develop spiritual friendships between people and try to bring this into every encounter. We put great value on working in teams and practising as a community. So, the warm welcome I received on first entering the centre was part of the ethos of Triratna.

For a while I simply enjoyed the unusual feeling of being with people who accepted me and who were always happy to talk. It was enough just to feel part of something that wasn't to do with my work. As I chatted, I started to be more interested in Buddhism and, after some reflection, asked to join a study group.

This study group opened so many doors for me. The same people met together, with minor changes, for about six years. I was suddenly part of a small group with the shared interest of learning more about Buddhism. Study training in Triratna is well organized and comprehensive – and I loved it. But, even more importantly for me than the study aspect, it also exemplified Triratna aspirations about how to be with the same people over a long period of time and how to make connections with them.

To begin with it was hard. This was partly because I found the pressure of people difficult. The sensory input of several people having an animated discussion was challenging. I found myself tensing up and trying to block some of it out. However, as we learned how to listen to each other, there were fewer times when several people were talking at once. I learned by watching other people roughly how long it was good to talk for. I also learned how to leave space for other people in the discussion. I discovered how to live with the feeling that I'd missed the time when it was appropriate to say something (so sometimes I would not be able to say what I wanted).

One of the other group members was really empathetic, a 'heart' person, while I'm more analytical and a 'mind' person. We discovered, to our mutual delight, that we could start a conversation coming from completely different places but eventually meet in the middle. This is such a rich experience, we both learned different ways of seeing and the world felt brighter because of this. I was beginning to build the foundations for closer relationships with other people.

After studying for a year, I decided that I was a Buddhist and that I wanted to make a deeper commitment to Buddhism, so I asked to become a 'mitra'. The word 'mitra' is usually translated as 'friend'. I discussed this with order members, and they agreed this would be a good step. I then took part in a ritual, where I was introduced to the whole sangha and made the three traditional offerings of a flower, a candle and incense – so that my deeper commitment could be witnessed.

I've never found rituals easy, there are usually too many people in the room and the overstimulation of mantra chanting makes these events difficult for me. Normally I don't want to be in the room doing this but, in this case, it felt really important to be seen. I wanted to take part in this ceremony with other people. I did find the sounds and the pressure of people challenging but I knew why I was there, and I wanted to be there, so it was bearable.

Once I'd made this deeper commitment, I also realized that I would like to be ordained into the Triratna Buddhist Order so I entered the ordination training. Order members started to suggest that it would be good to build friendships with other people in the sangha as the Triratna Order is simply a network of relationships. To become an Order member, you have to build these links with other people; it's an integral part of being in the Triratna movement. That sounded a lovely idea, but I'd never had a friend and I had absolutely no idea how to go about developing friendships. 'It's simple,' people said. 'You just have to ask.' Just ask...

If you are not autistic, maybe asking personal questions is an intuitive skill that you developed so long ago that you have forgotten you are doing it. You just ask and people respond. I was completely unable to proceed with this for some time. What should I ask? How should I phrase the question, so it wasn't a demand? How should I ask? Who should I ask? What if they said no? I just couldn't see how to do this. This felt very scary because I didn't know what to do.

The people around me saw me not responding to their

suggestion that I make friends. I believe they thought this was because I was choosing not to ask, and they were confused. Why wasn't I asking? I tried to explain but found it hard to say why. Eventually someone asked me if I would like to go for a coffee with them, and that was a huge relief. I made a note in my mind: you ask people to go for a coffee.

But the fact that I was going to meet someone for a coffee brought up a whole new area of difficulty – what do people do when they 'go for a coffee'? I'd never done this. I assumed that the idea was to talk, but talk about what? I was terrified. At that point I had no 'small talk'. I could not imagine how I was going to get through this meeting which felt so important. But I went, and it was very clunky. I could talk about non-specifics and we could discuss Buddhism, but I could not find any way of getting closer to the other person. I met other people after the first 'coffee experience' and it was clunky with everyone. The conversations just didn't flow.

At this point, many people would have given up on the idea of building a relationship with me. I was incredibly fortunate that the people here did not give up, as building friendships is the essence of being in Triratna. Instead, we kept meeting and people began to give me feedback about how talking with me felt for them.

At the start of this process the feedback was helpful. People said, 'You talk too much and don't let me get a word in.' So, I made a mental note to talk for less time and then pause, and this seemed to help. They said, 'You are too intense.' So, I tried to be gentler in the way I spoke and to give less detail. I tried to approach topics less directly (I didn't need that but the people with me did), so I put effort into softening my speech.

But as time went on and we still weren't really connecting the feedback became more painful and confusing. I was given information such as 'You are not listening to me', which was confusing because I was listening, as hard as I could. I was told, 'You are not interested in me.' This was very painful. I was more interested in people than I ever had been in my entire life, and yet this wasn't coming across. I was told, 'You don't have empathy.' This was both painful and confusing because I know that I have lots of empathy and I was trying to express it. Why couldn't the people I was talking to see that?

This phase lasted for several years, with both me and most of the people around me getting more frustrated. Why couldn't I do what was being asked? Nothing seemed to work. At the same time, I was finding that with two people things seemed to be different. I now know that both these people had met autistic people before. They assumed that I was autistic but that I didn't know it. So, they didn't expect the sort of responses that most non-autistic people were looking for. Our friendships developed more quickly because of this and they remain two of my closest friends to this day. They accepted that I was doing everything possible to relate with them and we flourished together.

Then four years ago, when I was 60, my sister contacted me to say that she had just been diagnosed as autistic. I went looking for information to help her and found the best description of me that I'd ever seen. My first response was, 'But that can't be true!' When I thought of autism I thought of severely autistic people, and I knew that their experience was not mine. And yet, there was so much in the description of autism that did fit. I researched further and discovered the concept of the autistic spectrum and suddenly everything made more sense. It was possible for someone to be autistic but not be severely autistic. I did the self-tests and discovered that my scores were way above the threshold values for autism. So, I asked to be tested formally. I was diagnosed with what is now called 'level 1' autism (in the UK) and might previously have been called Asperger's syndrome.

That diagnosis was liberating, suddenly I understood what was going on and I had the information to explain why I was having problems with communication. I told the people around me immediately and from just about everyone I got the response, 'Oh, *that's* what it is!' Swiftly followed by, 'Then you are doing so well!' I sent them information about how autism affects communication and the ability to build relationships. I explained that I could not respond in the ways that they were expecting.

Immediately things opened out. We realized that I could not read their non-verbal communication accurately and so could not find the appropriate responses. We also realized that they often could not read my body language accurately as well. For example, when they thought that I was showing worry or anger, I was concentrating. Almost at once we began to develop genuinely deep friendships which have stood the test of time. And also, I've developed strategies for showing that I'm listening. One of the most useful is the phrase 'What I'm hearing is...'. I often use this phrase to check that I have understood what is being said. Often, I haven't understood, but that's fine – we can clear up any misunderstanding immediately. As a result, people have started to say that I am a good listener, and that is precious to me.

Now I can truthfully say that I have many friends and some of these relationships are close, intimate friendships. We can talk about anything. It's just wonderful! It's taken so much time and effort from me and other people. This has happened because other people were prepared to put the time and effort in – because of their Buddhist beliefs and the ethos of the Triratna Order. I am now an Order member and sometimes I still can't believe that this is possible. I have so much gratitude towards Buddhism and the Triratna approach to Buddhist teachings. They have changed my life for the better.

CHAPTER 13

The Challenges of Engaging with Sangha

How Sanghas Can Develop More Inclusive Practice

ELEANOR LLOYD (*Dhiraprabha*)

The sangha, at its best, values kindness and respects the unique-ness of people. The Triratna Buddhist Community in particular practises friendship, which makes it an ideal context for anyone longing to engage more deeply with others. My own experience of autists engaging with sangha has been predominantly within the Triratna Community. I have witnessed many people deepen their commitment to the Triple Jewel through becoming 'mitras', then asking and training for ordination and eventually joining the Order. Among them have been some in middle age who, in the absence of a childhood diagnosis of autism, grew up with alternative labels such as obsessive, over-anxious, unsocia-ble or alcohol dependent. Most of these people became aware they were autistic due to increased self-awareness on the path towards ordination, often because of difficulties encountered. In sharing here some of the challenging aspects of five people's stories, including my own, without reference to the contexts of friendship and spiritual growth in which they are embedded, I present a partial and negatively weighted impression of sangha.

However, this is not my intention and I do so simply to identify areas where a better understanding of autism can alleviate
suffering. To protect anonymity, I have changed all names and
some details of situations encountered.

I was ordained into the Triratna Buddhist Order in 2002,
five years before receiving a diagnosis of autism, and the sangha
has become my spiritual home. As a child I experienced intense
loneliness which later combined with existential doubt to pre-
cipitate a moment of suffering-induced self-surrender. This was
a watershed moment for me as my despair and prayer were
simultaneously overwhelmed by the reality of unconditional
love. With this foundation, Buddhist practice and acceptance
within the sangha has enabled me to become more aware of
habitual anxiety and judgement in myself and to value connecting beyond the conceptual. I choose to call myself an autist and
celebrate the gift of my autism since without it I may never have
had the experience that gave rise to my faith or the motivation
to seek and follow a spiritual path. My heartfelt wish is for all
people, including autists such as Jonathan, Bobby, Beth and
Jo about whom I write, to be warmly appreciated within the
sangha and for the challenges involved to be better understood.

Feeling at home in the sangha depends initially on how one
is welcomed. When I arrived at my first Buddhist meditation
class, I was approached by a well-meaning person who had
noticed that I was a newcomer. She asked me about my experience of Buddhist practice, and I said, with autistic bluntness,
that I was a Christian. Taken aback she told me that the class
was not for Christians, and I assumed she wanted me to leave.
Fortunately, although feeling unwelcome, my desire to find out
about the Dharma was so strong that I continued to attend. I
wrote my request to become a mitra with care, detailing all my
reasons but without regard for the non-theistic perspective of
my audience. My request was refused, and the rejection was

painful and confusing for me. I did not want to pretend or lie about my faith in God, yet I believed the only way I could become more Buddhist was through engaging in the Dharma course known as 'mitra study'. Being determined by nature I persisted; other misunderstood autists have not. Some have remained on the fringes of sangha for a very long time in the absence of an appropriate invitation to become more involved.

For Jonathan, this period of partial engaging at his local Buddhist centre lasted two decades. He wrote to me, 'After 19 years I find myself very much wanting to become a mitra – but also having an immense struggle with the process of doing so.' The main obstacle was the nature of the traditional mitra ceremony: a seven-fold puja at a public event. Taken literally, it is untruthful speech to repeat verses of the puja such as, 'As many atoms as there are in the thousand million worlds so many times, I make reverent salutations.' And, 'What is not good, O Protectors, I shall not do again.' Consequently, some autists find this kind of poetic devotional language neither meaningful nor ethical and they cannot participate in it wholeheartedly, if at all. For Jonathan to be authentic at his mitra ceremony it was necessary for the simply worded three-fold puja to be used. Also, to prevent being overwhelmed by a crowd, the celebration needed to be limited to a small group of sangha members he knew well.

Jonathan identified as a non-binary person and found the division of study groups into men and women problematic. This is not uncommon for autists. In my own case I am more comfortable identifying as a person than as a woman, a fact I attribute to being unaware growing up of the subtler influences of female social conditioning. Jonathan explained to me that he much preferred discussing Dharma with women since he experienced men's communication style as argumentative. Jonathan was eager to do mitra study but there was no mixed-gender group he could be part of since the course was made available through men's or women's study groups. He joined the men's group but found himself resorting to silence whenever the men's group slipped into 'argument mode', hoping someone would eventually notice his non-participation and enquire. Regular attendance was difficult to sustain because the competitive verbal exchange exhausted him. Unlike other mitras in his group Jonathan decided that it was not possible for him to ask for ordination. The challenges were too great. He could not imagine coping on the men-only retreats which are central to the ordination process or being ordained into the 'men's wing' of the Order.

For autists who do ask for ordination, participation in residential study retreats undoubtedly presents additional challenges. For example, picture Bobby: I see them staring at the notice board, hands deep in the pockets of heavy corduroy trousers while other newly arrived retreatants mill around greeting each other. Bobby is preoccupied with anxiety, wondering in which shared room they will find a bed in a corner where they can sleep with the window wide open to the winter night. Next day in the Dharma study group we are asked to 'report in'. What should one say to this group of unknown sangha members? The person in corduroys gives their name and plunges into a detailed description of a difficulty they're experiencing in their local sangha, an account additionally complicated by their care to avoid specifics that could compromise confidentiality. The suffering they describe is not reflected in their tone of voice. No one comments and the round of introductions continues. Bobby, whose sensory system needed strong stimulation to function optimally, did not enjoy the study due to the hours spent sitting with others in a room they experienced as sterile.

Yet for many years they persevered in attending retreats, motivated by the goal of ordination. They were deeply inspired by the Sangha Jewel and recognized the possibility of genuine friendship within the Order based on a common commitment to meditation and ethical living. Their enthusiasm for the altruistic dimension of Buddhism knew no bounds and they assumed all Order members shared this passion for spreading the Dharma. As I got to know Bobby better, I learned that they had established a meditation group in their home, since there was no local Buddhist centre, and wanted Order members to be involved in leading sessions. Unfortunately, this teamwork was not going well. Bobby's difficulty in seeing the wider context of situations and other points of view had led to misunderstandings, and their determination and compelling need to resolve problems through addressing them head-on was being perceived as unskilful, even malicious, in intent.

Bobby was one among several mitras I got to know at a time when their individual ordination processes within the 'women's wing' were losing momentum. In each case Order members were feeling challenged, frustrated by persistent misunderstandings and apparent lack of progress. I have known five situations where the special relationship between an autistic mitra and their would-be preceptor came to an end, which necessitated these mitras finding another Order member eligible and willing to ordain them. This is not an easy task for an autist. For example, Bobby had suffered rejection as a child and had had their trust broken multiple times through being emotionally immature and socially naive. In addition, their mastery of appropriate ways to interact in specific social contexts, such as their home, school or workplace, had been fraught with difficulties. They were having to learn by trial and error the unique inexplicable social norms of sangha, such as how to be a 'spiritual friend'. Bobby asked me for information about the type of relationship to have with a potential preceptor: are they more akin to an older sibling or a parent, a teacher or a therapist? They wanted to know how to communicate with them, such as what kind of things to tell them and what to ask them in return, how often to initiate contact and where best to meet.

Unlike people who have innate knowledge of how to relate to others, Bobby's social behaviour was achieved by internalizing a complex web of rules. Inevitably these did not always fit a new social situation, resulting in some clunky behaviour. The difficulty in their local sangha that Bobby had alluded to when reporting in on retreat was a mistake of this kind. They had used a formal methodology taught to them as a social worker to address an informal situation within the sangha. Although their motive had been skilful, it was not recognized as such and the consequences unfolded painfully for all concerned. For Bobby the stress became so intolerable that they felt their only option was to withdraw their ordination request. They were not alone in their decision; I have known two other mitras each of whom, after striving for nearly 20 years, decided likewise. The process, in their experience, was of goalposts being invisible and moving, and of themselves being a 'wrong' fit.

A particular challenge of the ordination training process is that the 'right' way of behaving is to be increasingly authentic, which, for an autistic mitra, means becoming aware of and choosing to shed aspects of their acquired social-survival mask. However, other sangha members may misunderstand this vulnerable authenticity when they see it and respond in ways that discourage it. For example, people have experienced as unnecessarily argumentative or pedantically literalistic a mitra's determination to seek truth and maintain accuracy. Despite my own autism awareness, I too have felt critical rather than receptive at times when witnessing autists talk about themselves in ways that sound arrogant, harsh or dismissive. Bobby's particular style of communication – which made frequent use of idiom, pictorial metaphor and an advanced vocabulary of unusual words – was often judged as fanciful and out of touch with their audience. Also, the intensity with which they shared themselves verbally and energetically could cause discomfort in the listener. Although in non-sangha contexts Bobby was able to mask and use 'small talk' to connect socially, they couldn't accept there was a need for what they considered 'useless speech' in a conversation between spiritual friends. It can be tempting for those of us concerned with maintaining a harmonious sangha to try to 'correct' the behaviours we find challenging, including those that surprise or shock us by not conforming to our expectations.

Sometimes a clear recommendation to implement a particular speech or behaviour pattern, such as greeting friends arriving at a sangha event and asking a question about their home life, or 'keeping in touch' with them by sending a card, has enabled an autist to become better understood and appreciated by others. Yet it is unrealistic to expect them to generalize such modifications to other aspects of their authentic behaviour, however similar situations may appear to be. Ongoing encouragement from well-meaning Order members to achieve this has resulted in stress, confusion and a sense of failure for the mitra that has fed the negative legacy of previous social inadequacy. Suggesting to an autist that they try to communicate more sensitively or act with more awareness of themselves in relation to others can be as unskilful as asking a sight-impaired mitra to try harder to see.

Just as 'social blindness' may result in an autist misunderstanding an interaction, so 'autism blindness' can cause other sangha members to misread an autist's behaviour. An example of this is Beth gaining a reputation for being reactive. Sangha members believed they had witnessed her 'storming out of a study group' when, in fact, what they had seen and heard was

Beth leaving the room suddenly without saying where she was going and closing the door noisily behind her. Collectively they had interpreted her behaviour as a volitional act motivated by anger. When I asked Beth about this, she explained that she had felt the need for a break so had decided to visit the toilet; she had not left in response to anything said in the group. Far from being reactive, Beth was being attentive to her emotional and sensory regulation in a social context and physical environment she knew was challenging for her due to her autism. She recognized her need to take a break and thought she should do so without interrupting the discussion. However, also due to her autism, she assumed the group would know this, so she omitted to follow the social rule of telling them what she was doing and why. Her autism-associated dyspraxia accounted for her banging the door, along with her lack of realization that the noise could disturb and alarm people.

Another example is Jo not being taken seriously when she talked about her Dharma and meditation experiences. I listened in on a conversation Jo had with her prospective preceptor and heard a mismatch between the sincerity of the words she was speaking and the apparent flippancy of her tone of voice. She may have learned to minimize the effect of her communication in this way as a protection from making social blunders, but the habit was not helpful in the sangha. When she repeated her words with a deeper slower voice her open-hearted sharing was undisguised and thus better appreciated. The preceptor also told me how an understanding of autism had helped her to resolve another communication puzzle that had been complicating Jo's training for ordination:

I dubbed it language amplification: Jo amplified what people said, making it more black and white or extreme, looking for rules. When asked questions face to face that were either general or abstract,

Jo's answers were random, or off the wall, leading Order members to think she wasn't 'ready' for ordination. They heard her replies – especially if they were anxious replies to spontaneous questions where she was trying to guess what they wanted to hear – as more factual than they were. Following our discussion, I was able to ask the Order members to break a question down into more specific sub-questions, and give them to Jo 24 hours ahead so she had time to think about them.

Conversations such as these have led to a greater awareness of autism within the sangha in recent years. Quite frequently now I am asked by Order members, 'We think this mitra could be autistic, so should we tell them?' I imagine the Buddha would reply, 'If it is true, beneficial and timely, then yes.' I will add, 'If labelling precedes understanding, then no.' Knowledge of autism is often limited to the medical model of disability, and for a mitra to hear others are judging them in this way is very hurtful. The solution in my experience has been a gradual approach in which the mitra, their sangha friends and preceptor explore relevant information about autism together.

Studying the online training module 'Women and Girls' (National Autistic Society, UK) has proved especially useful for women in the sangha. Meantime, Order members are able to put their growing understanding of autism into practice and see if this helps the mitra they are concerned about. For example, Jo's preceptor felt that the culture of ordination training retreats did not meet Jo's learning and social style: 'All that togetherness, long group sessions, noisy dining room and shared bedrooms.' So she suggested offering her a single bedroom, an option to have meals alone, less time spent in large study groups and more specifically focused discussion. An informed recognition and empathetic accommodation of a mitra's particular needs is a kinder and more creative way to proceed than asking them if they are autistic.

At some point, though, an accurate diagnosis of autism is likely to be helpful for all concerned. For me personally, the initially painful challenge to my self-view was hugely worthwhile. Full acceptance was like the gift of a mirror to show me who I am in relation to others in a completely new non-judgemental way. For those familiar with Winnie the Pooh, I realized that I sometimes resembled Tigger bouncing up against Eeyore, and that this was not an occasion for blaming either myself or the other but an opportunity for a greater understanding of both. I remember a time a few years after my diagnosis when I confessed to my Chapter of trusted sangha friends that I made mistakes. I was shocked when they said they already knew that. I had believed that to have friends I needed to appear perfect and that I only had such good friends due to succeeding in this – hence the endless 'shoulds' and 'oughts' by which I lived socially. The relief of being able to take off this mask, knowing my friends loved me regardless, was incalculable. Challenges continue to arise as I engage with sangha but now, instead of facing these alone, I turn towards them with the support of spiritual friends. Through our better understanding of autism in the sangha, it is my hope that this may be so for everyone.

CHAPTER 14

Unsocially Social

The Benefits of Practising Online for Autistic People

BARRY TAYLOR

The evening before writing this I joined various other lay and ordained Buddhists for a session of chanting, meditation and teaching led by one of the monks from Buddhapadipa Temple in Wimbledon, London. In a few weeks' time I shall be participating in a three-day retreat at Amaravati Monastery in Hemel Hempstead led by lay teachers, and in a few months' time I shall be attending another Amaravati retreat led by the Abbot, Ajahn Amaro.

Why is this significant enough to warrant writing about? After all, I'm hardly the first Buddhist to participate in such activities. Well, it's significant because I'm writing this in the middle of a global coronavirus pandemic and because I live in a small town called Pontllanfraith in the South Wales Valleys, 156 miles away from Buddhapadipa Temple and 162 miles away from Amaravati Monastery. The current lockdown rules here in Wales don't allow me to leave my home for any non-essential reason, so the fact that I can participate in such activities from home via online streaming services makes a huge difference to me in terms of my ability to participate in group practice.

Of course, I'm not unique in this regard. At the moment the only real option for any Buddhist who doesn't live in a monastery to continue with any form of communal practice is to do so online. All over the world, Buddhist temples and monasteries have taken the giant leap of moving their teaching and practice sessions online using such platforms as Zoom, Teams, YouTube and Facebook Live. Thousands of us benefit from these technological solutions every day. In my case, though, I would be very happy for this form of practice to continue in some form even after the pandemic is over. You see, I am autistic.

I was diagnosed as autistic at the age of 46, by which time I had already been a Buddhist for several years. After a lifetime of struggling to come to terms with why I was different to others, of trying to fit in and trying to be 'normal' (whatever that means), I finally had a name for what made me the way I was. With greater self-understanding came greater confidence, along with a desire to learn more about myself and about how being autistic affects the way I see the world. It is well known that many autistic people develop special interests, or what could be uncharitably described as obsessions with rather obscure niche topics, and I'm no different. After my diagnosis, autism itself became a special interest for me and I read everything I could on the topic. I wanted to educate myself, to learn more about this condition that was such a huge part of what made me who I was, yet about which I knew relatively little. One thing that I discovered is that many autistic people have difficulty fitting in socially and could feel very uncomfortable in large groups. That came as no surprise to me because that was my own lived experience too.

Many times, I have found myself standing on the periphery of a group of people, not able to join in because I didn't understand the social cues well enough to know when to say something and when not to and wondering why I was even there in the first place. I am in awe of neurotypical people's ability to join in a conversation and become part of a group so seemingly effortlessly. The one time I can remember genuinely fitting in with a group in such circumstances was at an educational conference some years ago, where I noticed that a few people near me were speaking to each other in the Welsh language. As a Welsh speaker myself all I had to do was open my mouth and introduce myself and, in a hotel function room otherwise filled with people who were all speaking English, I was instantly accepted as one of the group – as an insider marked by my membership of the minority that they themselves belonged to. I have since found similar acceptance when I am with a group of fellow autistic people; I am part of a group of friends that met on a post-diagnostic course for adult autistics. We call ourselves the Autistibuddies and whenever we meet up we just understand each other in ways that none of us really ever get to experience when we are with non-autistic people. In most social situations, however, I freely admit that I'm about as much use as a chocolate teapot!

I remember the first time I ever walked into a Buddhist temple. I wanted to learn how to meditate because a therapist who was treating me for Post-Traumatic Stress Disorder (PTSD) had recommended it as something that could be helpful to me. She gave me a leaflet advertising beginners' meditation classes on Sundays at Palpung Changchub Dargyeling, a Tibetan Buddhist temple in Brynmawr, Blaenau Gwent. This was only a few miles away from both my home and my workplace, so it was quite easy to get to – but still I agonized over whether or not to go. The problem was that I had never been in a Buddhist temple before and I didn't know what to expect. I emailed the temple and got a friendly reply from the office manager, so I decided to give it a try. When I turned up for the first time, I knew nothing about Buddhism and everything felt very alien, despite the people being very friendly and explaining things to me. I was so nervous as I walked into the shrine room for the first time that my hands were actually shaking! Luckily for me though, I found the meditation teaching and practice very beneficial and so I continued going to the classes every week. Eventually I decided to become a Buddhist myself and I took refuge in the Buddha, Dharma and Sangha under the guidance of Chöje Lama Rabsang, the temple's resident monk and teacher.

I also wanted to learn about other forms of Buddhism, and one day a friend of mine who had lived in Thailand invited me along to the Thai Theravada temple that he had been attending. The temple was called Sanghapadipa Temple and at the time it was in Rhymni, which was also within a fairly easy driving distance from home for me. I took to Theravada Buddhism straight away. It was a better fit for me in terms of practice and beliefs, and though I kept my links with the Tibetan Buddhist community I became a regular attendee at Sanghapadipa Temple. There were several Thai monks in residence there, with varying levels of understanding of English. They were a little out of place in a strange culture by virtue of being from another country with very different social norms, whereas I was out of place by virtue of being autistic; this gave us a kind of common awkwardness which made it very easy for me to feel at home in their presence. Most of the lay practitioners I met at the temple were Thai as well, which was very different to the Tibetan Buddhist community since the latter was made up mostly of Westerners. The senior monk gave me the refuges and precepts and I committed to Theravada practice until, first, I became ill and couldn't attend for a while, and then, second, the temple moved to Swansea, which is a considerably longer drive away from where I live.

I started going more regularly to the Tibetan temple again for the sake of convenience, even though my personal practice was more in line with the Theravada way of doing things. This worked for a while, but then the unthinkable happened and a devastating global pandemic forced all in-person group activities to stop completely. Suddenly everything else seemed far less important as we all realized that we were now living through a major historical event that many of us would not survive. My wife and I both caught the virus quite early on and both of us were severely ill. Waiting for over ten hours for an ambulance while you are struggling for breath is a very effective way of bringing into sharp focus the Buddhist teachings on the brevity and fragility of life! The three marks of existence, namely Anicca (impermanence), Dukkha (suffering and unsatisfactoriness) and Anatta (not-self), become very clear at such extreme times. Eventually we both recovered from the immediate effects of COVID-19, though its long-term effects were still very much in evidence many months later.

After I had recovered from the worst of the COVID-19 infection enough to engage in group practice again, I discovered that the Tibetan temple was planning to start live-streaming its meditation classes and pujas via the media of Zoom and Facebook Live. I joined in these and, once I had got used to the new way of doing things, rapidly became comfortable with participating in group practice online while also continuing with my private practice at home in a way more in line with the Theravada tradition.

Fast forward a few months, and I found myself looking for more online Buddhist content. At this point I had a sudden realization that may seem obvious to many people but took a long time to hit me: since everything was now online, I didn't have to restrict myself to local groups anymore. I could join in with groups that had previously been inaccessible due to distance. A quick Google search revealed that not only were there plenty of options for online Buddhist practice and teaching, but many of them were from the Thai Theravada tradition with which I had such an affinity. Buddhapadipa Temple in Wimbledon, Amaravati Monastery in Hemel Hempstead and several others were offering online teachings, online meditation and chanting sessions and even online retreats. There were even revered monks as far away as Thailand offering Dhamma teaching in English online! I began to take advantage of these opportunities, along with listening to Buddhist teachings via podcasts from renowned teachers from all over the world. Now, not only can I practise my own meditation and chants at home as before, but I can receive teachings from, and ask questions of, insightful and accomplished teachers with no geographical barriers getting in the way.

As time has gone on, I have realized that in many ways the online practice environment is very well suited to me as an autistic Buddhist. For one thing, there is no pressure to maintain eye contact when the person with whom you are speaking is on a screen in front of you. As I, like many autistic people, find eye contact uncomfortable, the impact of even such a seemingly small thing as this cannot be understated. Also, if I find myself feeling uncomfortable because I can be seen by others, especially if I happen to be stimming, I can turn my camera off but continue to participate without being seen. As there are invariably other participants who also either turn their cameras off, or don't turn them on to begin with, this doesn't look odd to others and is accepted as normal behaviour in an online setting. This is so liberating for me as an autistic person because, unlike at in-person gatherings, I don't have to worry about controlling my stimming. I don't have to mask my autistic traits. I can be my true autistic self without fear of distracting others or being judged by them.

Although I am usually able to communicate verbally, there are times when I become non-verbal. This is not something I can control, and in many situations being non-verbal can be a significant hindrance when it comes to interacting with other people, especially in group settings. This is another situation in which online group practice can come to the rescue for those of us who are autistic. Every online medium I have used has a chat feature which allows you to type any questions or comments rather than make them verbally. Given that many people experience problems with slow internet connections causing them to be difficult to hear, using the chat function isn't regarded as unusual. Using it instead of speaking doesn't draw any unwanted attention to me, and so I don't stand out as unusual even when I am non-verbal. As a matter of fact, there are times when I prefer to use the chat function even when I am capable of verbalizing my questions and comments, simply because I am hyperlexic and so I am often more comfortable and fluent when I communicate in a text-based manner.

Like many other autistic people, I often struggle in unfocused social situations. I find it very difficult to hear what is being said when more than one person is speaking at a time, and I am terrible at making small talk as I have never seen the point of it. If you put me in a room with a group of strangers, I will be very easy to spot because I'll be the one on the periphery of the group, trying to follow what the others are saying but without much success. I will also probably be the only one who doesn't know what's happening. This is the natural habitat of the socially savvy neurotypical person; it is not where I feel at home. In online meetings, though, our roles can be reversed.

In my professional life I work as a language tutor, teaching Welsh to adults. Ordinarily this would take place in classrooms and other similar settings, but since the coronavirus pandemic hit the UK, we have moved all our lessons online. As a result, I have a lot of experience of using platforms such as Zoom in my professional capacity (for up to three hours at a time, in the case of the more intensive language courses). I feel comfortable with the environment. This is very much my domain, where people like me can feel more at home; you don't get multiple people speaking at once, since not only would autistic people not be able to hear them well, but neither would anyone else. This means that people in online groups tend to do more listening to others and tend to be more considerate of others in terms of not cutting them off or butting in as much. On the rare occasions when people are not quite so considerate, the online environments have a very handy feature that I often wish could exist in real life as well: the mute button! (This can, of course, be a bit of a pain as well – I think the two sentences I've spoken more than any others over the last year are 'Dych chi ar miwt' and its English equivalent, 'You're on mute.') Socially savvy neurotypical people might find the environment alien because of the tendency for there to be much less small talk and much more focused discussion, but that suits me fine. In fact, in many ways it brings out the best in me and allows me to contribute meaningfully to group discussions in a way that I never could in a real-life group in a physical room.

I have found online retreats to be very useful as well. I can follow the retreat timetable and participate in all the sessions without having to leave the familiar, comfortable surroundings of my own home. I'm fortunate to have a spare bedroom that I have converted into a personal shrine room, and that's where I do most of my sitting meditation and puja chanting in my day-to-day life. It's a calm and quiet space, and as such it's ideal for online retreats. There's even enough room for me to do walking meditation. When the time comes for teaching, I can listen via my laptop, and I can join in small group discussions on Zoom with ease. Then when I'm doing sitting or walking meditation, I just turn off the camera and set a timer for the end of the session so that I can be back at my laptop in time for the next session. No social pressures, no need to mask my autistic traits and no judgement. Honestly, I wish I'd been able to do this years ago!

There is, of course, the question of what will happen once life returns to some semblance of normality after the coronavirus pandemic. Undoubtedly some groups will go back to in-person meetings and completely stop their online provision, but personally I think this would be a mistake. Online provision enables not only people from a wider geographical area to benefit from teachings and group practices, but also those who have physical difficulties and are otherwise unable to visit a temple. Buddhist groups may also find that if they continue their online provision, more autistic people like myself will be able to participate more fully in Buddhist activities. Some may even discover the Dhamma for the very first time through such means, and that would be a wonderful and noble use of the technology.

I don't for one moment suggest that Buddhist groups should keep doing only online activities at the expense of their in-person activities. That would be ridiculous. I do think, however, that it would be a very good idea for them to set up a camera at the back of the room when they hold in-person events, perhaps with a connection to Zoom on a laptop next to the teacher so that online participants can ask questions as well. Such arrangements shouldn't interfere with the in-person activities, particularly as the necessary technology is now so small and unobtrusive, but they could make the difference between autistic people (and others) engaging with the Dhamma or deciding not to do so because of the very real physical and psychological barriers that might otherwise get in the way. The 'silver lining' of the global coronavirus pandemic for me has been the discovery by Buddhist groups and others that online practice can not only work but work very well. I hope this lesson will be one that won't be forgotten when things return to whatever may come to be regarded as normal in the post-pandemic world.

Greater awareness of the needs of autistic people would make the world a far better place to live for all of us, whatever our neurotype. This holds true for Buddhist communities as much as for any other part of society. Greater inclusion of autistic people gives us a chance to show how much of an asset we can be to any group, and online facilities have now become a big part of that. Long may such provisions continue!

CHAPTER 15

Community and Wellbeing

Everyday Life in a Zen Buddhist Temple

JOY TOBER

Peculiar smells, ringing bells, the steady melodic tones of chants, and, of course, lots of bowing. The wonderous world of a Buddhist temple can, to some, be an enchanting and inviting space, but to others it is an unknown and intimidating place of strange customs with unfamiliar forms and traditions. I remember the first time I walked through the doors of the Houston Zen Center to attend a meditation class; the rich aroma of incense evoked a sense of calm but the strange statues on ornately decorated alters gave me pause.

For me, my determination to find solace overruled my inner need to flee the unknown but that is not always the case for everyone, especially those diagnosed with an anxiety disorder, depression, or autism. Stepping into a new environment with unknown people, not knowing what to expect or what will happen next, can be astronomically alarming. My daughter was diagnosed as autistic at the age of four and I learned that her strong reactions to new places were due to her anxiety, her sensory sensitivities, and her difficulty processing new information and we both had to figure out how best to deal with these challenges; we are still learning. So, I was delighted when presented with the opportunity to write a chapter for this book from the perspective of someone who helps to create a space so everyone can feel included and welcomed.

My experience with Houston Zen Center did not end with a meditation class; what kept me returning again and again was the overwhelming kindness and compassion I received from the sangha and a sense of belonging I had never felt before. Now, as the administrator and volunteer coordinator at the center, I get the honor of being able to offer this same compassion and kindness to all those looking for a refuge from their suffering. Creating a healing space for those seeking comfort and peace can be a monumental task. However, by cultivating loving kindness, compassion, and supporting a beloved sangha alongside our devoted Abbot, our ardent residents and all the dedicated and caring members of the center help us to achieve this goal. Here are my experiences with Houston Zen Center that I feel help us to build a safe and sacred place for everyone.

The loving kindness practiced at Houston Zen Center is one of the things I cherish most about our center. Our purpose is to provide a safe space that supports the spiritual practice of Zen Buddhism and we do so by creating an environment free of judgement and filled with loving kindness. Whether it be the small gesture of offering a support cushion, making the effort to walk across a room to welcome an apprehensive new person, or just listening deeply to one another, our intention is for us all to be happy and free from suffering.

At this point I must confess I didn't know much about practicing loving kindness when I first came to work here. I am thankful for the lesson I was given years ago that has since allowed me the opportunity to offer my full loving kindness to everyone I encounter at the center. Our Abbot, Konjin Gaelyn Godwin, tirelessly leads an introduction to the Zen meditation course on a continuous basis. Although it is offered multiple times throughout the year, it nevertheless attracts a large group of students at each new offering. I had the great opportunity to help assist Gaelyn Roshi with this class for a few years after I started working at the center. In fact, this was the same class that introduced me to Houston Zen Center, so I was a little nostalgic and excited to be in a position of observance rather than participant. As Gaelyn Roshi's assistant I expected my job would be to merely welcome people into the center, direct them to the classroom, maintain the registration, and of course support the Abbot with anything she needed. Little did I know that in the course of helping I would be given the most precious gift of truly understanding the practice of loving kindness.

It is unfortunate that I am one of those people who has difficulty recalling names, a flaw I have come to accept but dislike, nonetheless. Gaelyn Roshi, on the other hand, has an amazing memory and a fascinating ability to recall just about anyone's name. I remember my surprise when I was a student that she remembered my name, and I then delighted in the fact that I might now learn her 'trick' as her assistant. However, what I quickly came to understand is that it is no trick at all but rather an act of loving kindness. When Gaelyn Roshi meets each student, she does so fully, taking in the whole person and being only with them in that moment. As her assistant, I tried this approach and found I was not as successful.

Although I tried my best and made notes to remind myself of each student's name, it just did not work. Speaking to Gaelyn Roshi one day before class, I mentioned my difficulty in recalling the names of the students. She told me that it helped her to recall each person every day, hold their image in her mind, and send good thoughts that the practice they were learning would help ease their suffering. So, the next day I sat at my desk with the registration list in my hand and went down the list one name at a time. I concentrated hard on each person, spoke their name, took a deep breath, and sent my hopes and wishes that whatever they learned during the class would allow their suffering to ease, if even for just a moment.

I did this every day for a week before the next class. As the students walked in and I could recognize each one, I began to feel a sense of interconnectedness I had not encountered before. I could see myself in each person, and them in me. As soon as this door was opened, I was able to observe this connection happening throughout the center, between senior members and newcomers, old Dharma friends, teachers, and students. It is this loving kindness cultivated over the years and extending itself to all those who wish to join us that exudes throughout our center and invites in all beings who wish to be free from suffering. No matter their background or abilities the door to liberation is available to them and they can find it here with us.

When I think of compassion, I am reminded that Thich Nhat Hanh once said that one compassionate word, action, or thought can reduce another person's suffering and bring him joy. When I think of compassion within Houston Zen Center what immediately comes to mind are those little, seemingly insignificant moments of helpfulness between long-time practitioner and beginner.

I receive a lot of emails and phone calls from people new to the center wanting to join in on one of our meditation periods or try a one-day sitting. Some are eager and excited while others are anxious and unsure. But they all ask the same question, 'What do I do when I get there?' Trying to explain the bows, the chants, and the forms would be overwhelming so, instead, I encourage them to look to someone who knows what they are doing. I ask them to remember that everyone in the room was once new and advise them that when in doubt, just bow. And finally, I reassure them that there will always be someone there to help.

Some of my favorite memories at the center are the ones in which an oversight was made or a misstep taken by myself or others, because it is in these moments that compassion blossomed and a connection was formed. Those of us who are now familiar with the forms and functions of the zendo can probably think back to our first zazen or one-day sitting and remember those first mistakes. This was when it was all new and unknown: the forgotten bow, the dropped utensil, or walking 'kinhin' in the wrong direction. These moments are probably not ones we will forget. But I always wonder, do we remember who was there to help show us the way?

My first one-day sitting is one I will not soon forget; it was to be my first 'oryoki' experience as well. About a week before the sitting, I had been given a little booklet of instructions which I read and reread obsessively. I had also taken a lesson from a resident who went through the entire ritual; so, on the day of the sitting I was confident I knew exactly what to do. During breakfast I opened my oryoki, placed the drying cloth and utensil holder in front of me, laid out my bowls, and then froze. My mind went completely blank, my heart began to race, a thin layer of sweat sprung up over my entire body, and I could feel my ears turn red. I had absolutely no idea what to do next. I looked up and saw everyone moving effortlessly through the motions and desperately tried to recall what step came next. As I scanned around the room looking for clues, I caught sight of someone staring at me. A senior member, who was sitting across the room from me, raised her eyebrows and smiled. She held up her utensils' holder and nodded at me. I took a deep breath and my heartbeat began to slow as I realized she was showing me what to do next. She patiently and compassionately walked me through each step without saying a word.

I enjoy sharing this story, one of my many follies, because this happens all the time in our center and I love it. I know for those in the midst of that moment it can be mortifying. But rest assured it is a moment many of us enjoy because we get to give comfort and confidence to others through our compassion. We embrace the chance to show others that they are welcomed and accepted just as they are, for we are all just humans.

It wasn't too long ago that my daily work tasks included updating registrations for classes, preparing our center for a weekend retreat, or creating announcements for our upcoming events. But one day in March of 2020 it all came to an abrupt stop when COVID-19 began to spread across the USA. An unexpected and frightening pandemic had descended upon the entire world and the center had to close. Our classes stopped meeting, our guests canceled, and our focus turned towards our sangha. How on earth were we to maintain the bond we had built for many years at such a long distance? And how were we to extend a helping hand to all those who would need it if our doors were quite literally shut? We knew the suffering that was happening around us and could foresee the intensity ahead, so it was with great love, kindness, and compassion that we decided to make every effort to stay connected to both our sangha and the world.

Our focus first centered on the wellbeing of our beloved sangha, so we decided to create a sangha buddy system. Gaelyn Roshi, a few senior members of the center, and I sat down with a list of all our members and friends and gathered contact information on everyone we could think of and paired long-time practitioners with newer members. Our goal was to give each person a lifeline of sorts and a way to stay connected to the sangha and the center. As I sat typing up messages to send my mind began to create an image of our center. Every time I hit send, I imagined a string, one end tied to the center and the other flying out to each person, until hundreds of strings extended far and wide from our building, each person tethered to us. For some, this tether was one of few connections they had to a world outside their home. And for others, it was a comforting reminder that should they need us, we would always be there. We didn't want anyone to feel as if they were facing this alone.

Once we knew our sangha was taken care of, we decided to try and figure out a way we could continue to offer a refuge to others. It just so happens a few months before the entire country shut down, Gaelyn Roshi had begun working with what was then a new online platform called Zoom. Who knew this would become the link that would connect us all? Over the next few months Gaelyn Roshi, along with our residents Royce Johnson and Vicki Glenn, set up our Cloud Zendo, our connection to the world. Here we invited everyone into our virtual zendo to practice together. People from all over the world joined us and we began to form relationships and friendships with people we never would have met otherwise. Building upon this, we started to offer retreats, brought back our classes, hosted Dharma talks with new teachers, and even continued our summer practice period – all virtually and all filled with the same dedication, compassion, and love as before. I have received a good number of messages thanking us for our continued presence and it fills me with joy to know that our efforts to continue the Dharma during such a difficult time were able to bring comfort to those seeking support and solace.

With vaccinations on the rise, the country has begun to slowly turn a corner on the pandemic, and we have happily opened our doors to visitors once again. As we continue to expand our offerings along a variety of pathways, we recognize the importance in continuing to offer a place of refuge and healing. If there is one lesson I have learned through this recent experience, it's that adapting to the current needs of practitioners is just as important as honoring the traditions of the past. With kindness and compassion, we at the center are dedicated to helping others relieve their suffering through the teaching and sharing of the Dharma and the considerate acceptance of all beings.

CHAPTER 16

Reflections

CHRIS JARRELL

It's not my place as the editor of this anthology of personal accounts of autistic Buddhists to make an analysis of what has been written or draw any conclusions about the potential benefits (or challenges) of Buddhist practice. The stories speak for themselves and, indeed, the submission guidelines for contributors asked that they did not finish their pieces with any conclusions, but allow you, the reader, to make up your own mind about how to proceed from here. Furthermore, I am not a Dharma teacher, nor am I an 'expert' on autism. But I do have lived experience of both the Dharma and autism – as an autistic man and as a practising Buddhist. And it is on this basis that I would like to take this opportunity to reflect on some of the benefits, and challenges, I have experienced that resonate with these accounts, and the conversations I have had with the writers during the editorial process. I would also like to share some of my experiences of teachers and sanghas that I hope will be of benefit to you as you begin to study the Dharma and explore what sangha possibilities are appropriate and open to you. In addition, if you are a Dharma teacher, centre director or practice group leader, then, rather than *instruct* you in how to develop your autism sensitive practice, I have provided a simple guide in Appendix I. This will help you to structure your discussions when it comes to working on your diversity agenda and improving accessibility for autistic people in your sangha.

One of the benefits of Buddhist practice that has struck a chord with me is the increasing ability of some of the writers to regulate their emotions. Pete Grella provides a good example of this when he tells the story of managing a panic attack in the middle of a mosh pit. My own learning has taken place over a number of years as my practice has deepened, and more recently as my understanding of autism has developed. It has grown against a backdrop of being kind to myself when my autism generates what I experience as overwhelming and debilitating emotions. These strong emotions are not always easy to explore during sitting meditation and it is sometimes necessary to take time out from sitting and just be mindful of how these feelings are impacting on my day, and how I am trying to avoid them or self-soothe by attaching to people or objects of desire. It is possible, for example, when eating too many snacks or watching too much daytime TV to still be in touch with Dharma! So instead of calling myself a 'bad Buddhist' because I am staying away from formal meditation, as soon as I feel able to, I return to sitting and following my breath. This may take some time as I find my way back to my meditation stool through, for example, mindful eating or walking meditation. As another example, Ish Tannahill's account describes how they have found a middle way of dealing with the difficulties of strong emotions through their friendship with a Buddhist Chaplain. Rather than engage in periods of meditation, they read and discuss sutras together.

Several writers in this anthology testify to how the Dharma, with the support of a sangha, has helped them to be more authentically autistic. I am a beginner in this area of my spiritual development. I had a very late diagnosis of Autism Spectrum Disorder (ASD) and so I am still working through my feelings about being a 'bad' neurotypical person rather than a good enough autistic person. I'm getting there slowly. Jessica Woodford writes convincingly about how her sangha helps her to be comfortable with her autistic self by accepting her for who she is. This helps her with confidence and self-esteem. It is accounts like this that are helping me in my journey to self-acceptance. Lian Beijers gives a clear description of how the Five Mindfulness Trainings give her 'permission' to be herself within a contemporary, young, neurotypical peer group that at times consume and behave in ways that she finds difficult to go along with. It may seem contradictory to some readers to read about how Buddhist practice can help us to be our autistic selves when one of the fruits of the practice is the realization of 'no-self'. But meditating on 'no-self' in order to dissolve our ego does not mean that we do not need an everyday self in order to live our lives. It is when our everyday self becomes the centre of our existence, to the exclusion of other people's feelings, that we start to have problematic thinking and difficult emotions that generate our suffering and contribute to the suffering of others. The Dharma teaches us how to dissolve the self that insists on 'ME!' being the focus of our attention. I am still learning to be aware of no-self when ME! feels threatened and reacts by being angry and melting down (or by becoming anxious and shutting down).

Autistic people lacking emotional empathy and the ability to develop a 'theory of mind' is a contentious area of debate. In my view, it may be the case for some autistic people, as well as some neurotypical people, but not for all of us. Indeed, many of the accounts in this anthology provide testimony to how the contributors have developed the ability to be more aware of other people's feelings as their Buddhist practice has deepened. The writers also record how, through the support of their sanghas, they are better able to acknowledge that other people in their lives have a point of view based on their own experiences, and consequently have needs of their own. Not everything and everyone revolves around ME! As my practice has deepened, and my sense of an autistic self has become clearer, I am learning to recognize that we are all interconnected at a fundamental spiritual level as well as in an everyday, mundane way. This knowledge strengthens my confidence to be empathic and act in a loving and kind way. I use the word 'confidence' purposefully because the strong sense of compassion I have always had, combined with a less developed capacity to be empathic, has often seemed at odds with the world in which I have been living. Louise Woodford, in her account, comments on the overwhelming compassion she has always felt and how learning about the Dharma has given her the confidence to be her authentic, compassionate, autistic self. My learning in this area of my life has also been possible because of a subtle and gradual shift from understanding the Dharma intellectually to feeling the Dharma at a deeper, personal level.

The benefits of being part of a supportive, like-minded community has been mentioned a number of times by writers, but there are difficulties in accessing these benefits for some autistic people. Jane Garratt has given an account of how her entry into a sangha over a period of years was not always easy, for her or the other members. Perseverance by all brought about a positive result despite a fundamental disconnect making for a challenging path to friendship for everyone. Jane's account suggests that a lack of knowledge of social skills on both sides of the neuro-divide can contribute to difficulties in forging supportive spiritual friendships. In my case, low self-esteem and a lack of confidence in making friends, another characteristic of some autistic people, has contributed to my difficulty in connecting within a sangha. Adding to the complicated mix of factors affecting friendships between neurotypical and autistic people within sanghas is a lack of knowledge of autism by administrators, teachers and sangha members.

My personal experiences of teachers and sangha have mostly been positive, but it only takes one negative experience for me to have to take time out to process thoughts and feelings in my own, individually autistic way. This takes time, and time away from a sangha may mean that I don't return. Sometimes this negative experience happens up front on my first visit and I don't get a chance to settle in. I am learning to be kind to myself when this happens. For example, I have found that one of the ways that neurotypical people learn about new places and groups is by engaging in small talk, getting to know people, sharing worries and uncertainties and looking for similarities between group members to build on. As an autistic person I have always found this difficult, and sometimes impossible, and usually get left behind in this process. I have witnessed other newcomers to groups seemingly effortlessly chatting away and becoming a part of a community relatively quickly. I have always been quick to judge myself and wish now I had been kinder by giving myself more time to settle in. But the exhaustion that comes with joining a group always made managing this process difficult.

There are some very practical things I wish I had known when I first started to attend workshops and classes. Dhiraprabha, in her account of supporting autistic people in settling into sanghas, mentions, for example, how disruptive it can be when someone leaves a room by slamming a door. This is something we are all likely to do inadvertently when upset or distracted. We all know that, as well as being very calming and relaxing, meditation can evoke difficult feelings and strong emotions. But instead of sitting and suffering in silence when this happens, try looking around you, think of something pleasant. If this doesn't work, leave the room and find a quiet space. Leaving a room during a meditation or in the middle of a Dharma talk can be challenging, especially when we are beginning to melt down or shut down. So, without trying to take any of your belongings (maybe just your bag if you really need to), try quietly standing and slowly bowing to the teacher with palms pressed together in front of your chest in a traditional prayer posture. Then walk slowly around the outside of the circle, or down the middle aisle, to the door, following your breath as you walk. Quietly open the door, remembering that some doors have minds of their own and may slam shut after you. Once out of the room, walk calmly and slowly to a quiet space.

I find centre bookshops and libraries are quiet spaces; failing that I head to the restroom. If you are taking a break during a class, the likelihood of someone banging on the door is small! If the weather is good, and I am in a safe neighbourhood, I sometimes take a walk round the block, or if there is a nearby park I sit for a while. If the weather is bad, I sit in my car. If there is a café, then a coffee always goes down well. The main thing I try and remind myself is that I am not behaving in an odd or unusual way. I am being kind to myself and, by caring for my feelings, I am maximizing the chances of me going back to the group. By the way, always keep a class schedule with you, either a hard copy or on your phone, so that you know the best time you can rejoin the group – maybe when it takes its next break. And, from a personal safety perspective, try and tell someone if you are leaving the centre.

Another practical thing I wish I had known when I started studying the Dharma was that you don't have to prostrate or chant when everybody else does. Different traditions have different rituals and ways of expressing their devotion. As an autistic person, I find some of these rituals resonate with my existing sense of respect for others. So, for example, if a group stands when the teacher enters the room, I am comfortable with that. In some Tibetan centres a bell rings when the teacher is about to enter the room and everyone stands. The teacher will prostrate three times in the direction of an effigy of the Buddha, and the class may prostrate as well. I will bow with my hands in the prayer position. This is what I feel comfortable with and that is OK. Again, if the group chants, I sit and listen respectfully and often find comfort and reassurance in the sounds of the voices around me. I just try to relax and let go of the feeling of being odd or different. I remind myself that all these people were newbies once.

One of my strengths as an autistic person is my naivety. This is usually seen as a negative characteristic in adults. However, my naivety, aside from being a source of difficulty over the years, has always helped me to see the best in people and believe in their capacity for growth and change. But I do have a tendency to accept people at face value and this is particularly noticeable in my experience of Dharma teachers. For me, a measure of a good Dharma teacher is their ability to be present in the moment and be aware of their students' needs in a loving and compassionate way. Authentic teachers will have a presence about them that you will connect with. An inauthentic teacher will be picked up by your autistic radar. They always say that you can make up your mind about someone within a few minutes of meeting them, and it is no different with Dharma teachers. Unfortunately, many Dharma teachers have a charisma that can mask their lack of authenticity and I have sometimes found myself in the position of the 'little boy and the emperor's new clothes'. I have benefitted immensely from listening to Dharma talks over the years, and from receiving the loving kindness and compassion of teachers. But I have also witnessed questionable situations where a teacher's ability to authentically transmit the Dharma to their students has been limited, to say the least. You will no doubt make up your own mind.

In the same vein, small groups are not always what they seem to be. Small group work can be challenging at the best of times. I remember the first retreat I went on – we split into small groups for Dharma sharing, and everybody started talking about anything and everything but the Dharma. I was shocked and frustrated. I withdrew emotionally and sat quietly as the small talk went on around me. What I didn't realize at the time was that because they had never been in a group together before, what they were doing was perfectly acceptable in terms of getting to know each other. The Dharma sharing would come later. I have now learned that a group discussion can be unpredictable and that I need to try and relax and, if possible, make a contribution that fits with the tone of the conversation or the stage that the group is at. My difficulty with this is that, unfortunately, by the time I have thought of something relevant to say, the conversation has moved on!

Most traditions are similar in that they have introductory courses. I have learned the hard way that it's a good idea to join one. I would not only have benefitted from the opportunity to learn the basics of Buddhism, but also have been able to meet people who would, like me, be new to the tradition. By participating in an introductory course, either in person or online, you will have a ready-made friendship group within the sangha. Leading on from introductory courses are classes, workshops and retreats that introduce Dharma students to deepening levels of meditation. Where traditions will differ is what methods of deepening meditation they teach and what eventual outcomes they lead to. For example, some traditions emphasize the transformation of difficult feelings and troublesome thoughts through deep listening and loving kindness. Other traditions will encourage you to purify yourself from past actions and deeds by accumulating merit. Some will aim for enlightenment for enlightenment's sake, others will aim for enlightenment for the benefit of all sentient beings. It's worth checking this out right from the start before investing your time and energy in an introductory course.

In the absence of a local centre, you will probably, like me, parachute into a programme of study by attending a weekend retreat or a day class (or maybe an online event) and be inspired to learn more. Making an emotional decision about a potential special interest is not always a bad thing, but remember that classes and sangha can be just as challenging as they can be inclusive and supportive. As the writers in this anthology have said, the Dharma makes 'perfect, logical sense' to an autistic mind. However, such clarity in what is often a confusing and overwhelming world can become, paradoxically, an object of attachment. By attaching too strongly we can become our own worst critic. 'I am not a good enough meditator. The way I earn my living conflicts with Right Livelihood. I must always practise compassion and loving kindness. I don't know the Sanskrit word for "meditation". Why did I say that, will people think I'm odd?' Finding a balance between absorbing ourselves in the Dharma and sangha and being kind to ourselves is not always easy. Especially when special interests can become very intense and all-consuming for some autistic people. Practising equanimity and finding the middle way has been difficult for me over the years and I wish now that I had paced myself more. However, 'pacing' is not something that autistic people associate with special interests!

Change takes time and is not always easy. When it comes to lifelong habits and new ways of thinking, feeling and behaving – well, it's even more difficult. Have you ever responded to an advertisement about nicotine patches and tried to give up smoking? You will see online advertisements by some Buddhist organizations promoting workshops that are about 'how to be happy'. Rather than the quick fix they may suggest, these workshops should introduce you to a lifelong path of study, reflection, practice and change. This can take time. In my case, with a tendency to depression and anxiety closely associated with my autistic self, I have had to take time out over the years to access more secular sources of support like medical services and counselling. I have been lucky enough to be able to integrate this kind of support into my Dharma practice. A good Dharma teacher will support you with this approach to finding community and wellbeing.

Take things slowly, stay in the moment and breathe through your difficulties. If you are not able to do that, then take some time out and try again later. After all, the Triple Jewel has been around for over 2000 years. The Triple Jewel patiently waits deep within us for the moment when the clouds clear from our essentially bright, empty and spacious minds, and we are able to smile at the world with loving kindness and compassion. By opening our hearts to the Dharma, accepting the support of spiritual friends and establishing a realistic and compassionate meditation practice that acknowledges our difficulties as autistic people, I believe this is possible. Don't forget, our capacity to undertake research, study diligently and commit to projects that are of special interest to us are among our strengths.

Taking a step from the secular use of meditation and mindfulness practices into the world of Buddhism may not be right for all autistic people. But with increasing diversity within sanghas becoming high on the agenda of Dharma teachers, meditation centres and practice group leaders, now may be a good time to take that next step and explore what the possibilities are. Particularly at a time when the opportunities for online participation are growing as a result of the global pandemic preventing face-to-face meetings. As Barry Taylor says in his piece, now could be the time to try being 'unsocially social'. And in doing so, you may well take the first steps towards learning about Buddhist communities and developing your spiritual wellbeing.

Contributor Biographies

Sian Atkins is a writer and visual artist whose interests span Buddhism, autism, queerness, self-help, anti-capitalism, music and travel. She previously studied geography, French and international development, and has worked in administration, research and teaching roles in the UK, France and Madagascar. She currently lives in Cardiff, Wales.

Dr Lian Beijers, who has recently finished her PhD in psychiatric epidemiology, began practising in the Plum Village tradition in 2019. She received the Five Mindfulness Trainings that same year and was given the Dharma name 'Courageous Connection of the Heart'. She went on to regularly facilitate meetings with her local sangha in Holland. Since writing her contribution for this anthology, Lian has been accepted as an aspirant for the five-year monastic training programme in Lower Hamlet, Plum Village.

Dr Pernille Damore is a Danish naturopathic doctor, psychomotoric therapist and published author. Her autistic interdisciplinary ability helps her to communicate complicated topics and consider parallels between themes. Her special interests are health, biology (especially biochemistry and endocrinology) and neurodiversity. She is also interested in meditation, non-duality mindfulness and the practical application of the Dharma. Pernille resides in Shropshire, UK.

Jane Garratt (*Prajnanandi*) is an ordained member of the Triratna Buddhist Community and has been a practising Buddhist for 15 years. She was brought up an atheist and worked as a scientist. Jane now thinks it is a joy to have found a spiritual way of living. At heart she is more attracted to the Pali Canon than to Mahayana approaches but thinks Vajrayana wisdom teachings are wonderful. She lives in south-east England with her husband.

Pete Grella is a Los Angeles based meditation facilitator empowered by InsightLA. He has been meditating and studying secular Buddhism for the past decade. He's attended numerous meditation retreats and workshops on Authentic Relating, communication and skilful intimacy. Pete is diagnosed with Autism Spectrum Disorder and, after experiencing his own transformation using the tools of Buddhist meditation, is an avid proponent of meditation as a resource for adults on the spectrum. He has a degree in Applied Mathematics from UCLA.

Danielle Hall is a passionate birder, ecologist, wildlife photographer, gardener and environmentalist. She is also active in human, animal and environmental rights. She is a full-time student and has just completed research on habitat fragmentation as it relates to birds. When her studies are complete, she plans to teach people about birding, ecosystems and regenerative gardening. She joined the 'Florida Community of Mindfulness' in December 2020 and feels incredibly at home with her beautiful sangha. Danielle lives in the Tampa Bay area of Florida with her husband, Brent, and their three lovely boys.

Chris Jarrell is a retired social work lecturer and counsellor who started his working life in the mid-1970s with people with a learning disability. He has a PhD in Gender Studies and an MA in Educational Studies, both from the University of Hull. Chris has a very late ASD diagnosis and calls himself a Buddhist nomad because he has been unable to settle with one tradition. He lives in Hull, East Yorkshire, with his very patient partner of 42 years, Sue, and enjoys being a grandad and working mindfully on his allotment.

Lucy Liu is a family advice and support worker with Skills for People in Newcastle (UK). She has an Autism MA from the University of Northumbria. Lucy is neurotypical but has a teenage autistic daughter. She practises Buddhism in the Plum Village mindfulness tradition. She is particularly interested in developing accessible ways of sharing the Dharma with autistic young people who otherwise would feel overwhelmed by the complexity of the teachings and the intensity of meditative practice.

Eleanor Lloyd (*Dhiraprabha*) grew up in an English Quaker family. Her lifelong passion has been inclusive child-centred education and she spent 30 years developing this in East London primary schools. She became Dhiraprabha in 2002 when she was ordained into the Triratna Buddhist Order and subsequently sought and received a diagnosis of autism. She has Master's degrees in both religion and autism and enjoys meeting autistic people on the spiritual path. Currently she lives in Aotearoa, New Zealand.

Dena Rashkover (*Piyadithha*) is a free-spirited special needs teacher and Dharma practitioner residing in the mountains of North Carolina. She integrates socially engaged Buddhism into her work in a public elementary school setting. She has been teaching young children with significant, multiple needs, including those on the autism spectrum and cognitive impairments, for 28 years. It is not her work, but her passion and calling. Each child is a true teacher of kindness and compassion, rooted in their own nature. Dena is a member of Heartwood Refuge Center and enjoys nature, hiking, reading, crosswords and being one with the universe.

Ish Tannahill (they/them) is from Cambridge, England, and first came to Buddhism through Triratna. They have, however, recently moved to a sangha facilitated by Plum Village. Ish previously had roles working in charities and working as a receptionist in a healthcare environment. They are currently studying an Access to Higher Education course and looking to study Social Psychology as a degree. Despite the challenges of several mental and physical disabilities, they are looking forward to their degree and future working life.

Barry Taylor is a part-time primary school teacher and adult Welsh language tutor from Pontllanfraith, South Wales. He was diagnosed as autistic at the age of 46. A theologically educated former Christian, Barry practises with both the Thai Theravada and the Tibetan Vajrayana traditions. Although at heart he is a Theravada Buddhist, he finds great benefit in both traditions and appreciates the breadth of wisdom that can be accessed by having teachers from two such different lineages.

Joy Tober is the administrative assistant and volunteer coordinator at Houston Zen Center and has been practising Buddhism in the Soto Zen tradition for eight years. Although trained in historic preservation, Joy found working to help others along the path to end suffering was an opportunity she could not pass up. Joy is the proud mother to her autistic daughter who brings light and bliss to her world every day. She resides in Houston, Texas, with her husband, Rich, their daughter, Ruby, and their two quirky cats.

Jessica Woodford, age 11, is an aspiring author and a musician. She plays piano and is working towards her grade 6 in clarinet. She also plays saxophone and clarinet in a marching band, regularly performing gigs in front of thousands of people. Her favourite hobbies include art, yoga, athletics and of course spending time with her turkeys! She and her best friend (aka her brother) enjoy nature, camping in their campervan and composing/playing music together.

Louise Woodford and her family enjoy a home-educating life-style. She and her husband run two small businesses from their home in the south-east of England. However, they can often be found travelling the country in their campervan, visiting muse-ums, castles and other places of interest, thoroughly enjoying the freedom of no school! Louise began learning Buddhism with a Tibetan tradition before meeting and falling in love with Plum Village.

APPENDICES

APPENDICES

A Short Guide to Autism Sensitive Practice

This document can be used as a basis for discussion and action within your centre or practice group. It is not meant to be pro-scriptive, as different schools and traditions have different ways of facilitating teaching and meditation events. This guide is the result of a collaborative piece of work between the editor, contributors, Dharma centre directors, administrators and practice group leaders. Although no two autistic people are the same, just as no two neurotypical people are the same, there are identifiable and achievable changes you can make and build on to help autistic people access your centre or group.

I. **If you know any autistic people, try and involve them in discussions about guidelines for 'autism sensitive practice'.** You may not have any autistic people that you know of in your sangha or family and friendship groups, so consider reaching out via local autism support groups, which you can usually connect with via national websites (see Appendix III). There are also a growing number of autistic Buddhist practice groups such as Autsit that would be only too pleased to talk to you about including autism as part of your diversity agenda.

2. **Not all autistic people will tell you about their autism, so consider reaching out with a positive statement on your website,** together with contact details for a 'go-to' person. It's often difficult for an autistic person to share information about themselves because of previous experiences of discrimination and abuse, or they may be concerned that people may not believe them or discount their autistic traits as not important. So, the questions for us are always, 'Who do you tell?', 'Who can you trust to be discreet?'

3. **Make sure that the 'go-to' person in your organization, centre or group has undergone 'autism awareness' training (see Appendix III).** Some of the contributors to this anthology have explained that it was easier to relate to people within a sangha who had had some previous experience of autistic people. Participating on a course is not going to make you an 'autism expert' (if there is such a thing) but it will help to sensitize you to potential contact with autistic people (who may or may not know they are autistic themselves).

4. **When planning an event or practice group, be aware of potential sensory overload issues for autistic people** (and others) such as noisy breaks, iconography, chanting, bright lights and strong incense burning. It may be worth considering, for example, the benefits of installing dimmer switches and monitoring the brightness of the sunlight that is entering the room over the period of a session.

5. **Make available the protocols that you would normally expect people to observe whilst in the centre.** Every group or organization has 'hidden rules' that are only discovered by trial and error, and by becoming part of

the group, asking questions and receiving feedback. This is something that autistic people may find difficult. Listing the rules and making them available for all could be an interesting and useful exercise for all concerned. Include a 'go-to' person for any questions or advice. Consider how an autistic person may identify and approach that person.

6. **Some centres and groups have 'greeters' who say hi as soon as a new person walks in.** They explain everything (like shoes, restrooms, books and food) and help people to feel welcome. Autistic people would certainly benefit from this; it would greatly reduce their confusion and anxiety and help free up their energy to participate in the main event.

7. **Identify a quiet space where autistic people (and others) can take time to recover when feeling overwhelmed** by, for example, too much social interaction, the content of teachings and the depth of guided meditations. Libraries, bookshops and outside spaces could be designated as quiet areas – with a 'crash room' and a comfortable chair for people who need more immediate access to a quiet place.

8. **Notice people on the periphery of groups and conversations who seem socially awkward and seek out quiet spaces during breaks.** This doesn't necessarily mean they are autistic, but it can be an indicator. Consider reaching out. Conversely, some autistic people (and others) may be over-engaged, find it difficult to listen and take up a lot of space in teachings and conversations. Does your sangha have a protocol for managing difficult situations like this?

9. **Try and keep sessions to time.** Autistic people (and others) may be managing an overwhelm and waiting for the next break in order to calm down and self-comfort. Do you have an arrangement for prompting the speaker as the end time for the session approaches?

10. Usually there are exercises where people group up and talk about their experiences and their feelings. This isn't always bad for autistic people, **but they may find it difficult to join a group**. Looking out for people who are alone when everyone else is grouping up would be helpful, not only for autistic people but for other new people. Could the teacher help people pair up or form groups?

11. **Consider taking silent breaks from time to time**, mix them up with regular breaks (when neurotypical people can still have the opportunity to talk and socialize). This is not to say that autistic people necessarily dislike talking and socializing, but the sensory overwhelm can be too much, sometimes, to deal with.

12. **When introducing a meditation, give people permission to 'not complete' if they are beginning to feel overwhelmed.** Provide some guidance on self-care when difficult feelings arise, including how to leave the room quietly and respectfully (if they need to) and where the nearest place of refuge is.

13. **When a teacher asks someone a question during a session, and they appear to freeze or stumble, tell them it's OK to take some time to think about an answer**, and move on. Remember that autistic people need more processing time than neurotypical people and may react rather than respond if they feel under pressure to give an

answer. Consider coming back to them during questions and answers.

14. **It is easier for autistic people (and some others) to raise a hand to ask a question, rather than just call out.** A teacher facilitating people raising their hand and being called upon before they speak helps keep the group from being dominated by an extrovert and provides a safer space for all.

15. **Many autistic people benefit by having access to live, online streaming of events. Provide a two-way opportunity for autistic people to participate by asking questions** (either in comment boxes on the screen or in person) and provide a tech-savvy facilitator. Regarding the asking of questions, the teacher just saying 'just unmute yourself and ask a question' lends itself to autistic people being excluded. Consider facilitating participants to physically or virtually raise a hand and then being called upon to speak.

16. **If an individual doesn't come back after a session, consider a follow-up call and ask for feedback.** Many autistic people (as well as others) can feel overwhelmed by situations and encounters that most neurotypical people, by seeking the informal support of other sangha members, may take in their stride.

17. **Autistic people can be very direct and honest when they give feedback.** Consider how you or your organization may respond to this kind of communication style. Is your centre or group open to receiving feedback and does it have processes in place to respond appropriately?

The Five Mindfulness Trainings

Reproduced with the permission of Parallax Press: https://plum-village.org/mindfulness-practice/the-5-mindfulness-trainings

1. REVERENCE FOR LIFE

Aware of the suffering caused by the destruction of life, I am committed to cultivating the insight of interbeing and compassion and learning ways to protect the lives of people, animals, plants, and minerals. I am determined not to kill, not to let others kill, and not to support any act of killing in the world, in my thinking, or in my way of life. Seeing that harmful actions arise from anger, fear, greed, and intolerance, which in turn come from dualistic and discriminative thinking, I will cultivate openness, non-discrimination, and non-attachment to views in order to transform violence, fanaticism, and dogmatism in myself and in the world.

2. TRUE HAPPINESS

Aware of the suffering caused by exploitation, social injustice, stealing, and oppression, I am committed to practicing generosity in my thinking, speaking, and acting. I am determined not to steal and not to possess anything that should belong to others; and I will share my time, energy, and material resources with those who are in need. I will practice looking deeply to see that the happiness and suffering of others are not separate from my own happiness and suffering; that true happiness is not possible without understanding and compassion; and that running after wealth, fame, power, and sensual pleasures can bring much suffering and despair. I am aware that happiness depends on my mental attitude and not on external conditions, and that I can live happily in the present moment simply by remembering that I already have more than enough conditions to be happy. I am committed to practicing Right Livelihood so that I can help reduce the suffering of living beings on Earth and stop contributing to climate change.

3. TRUE LOVE

Aware of the suffering caused by sexual misconduct, I am committed to cultivating responsibility and learning ways to protect the safety and integrity of individuals, couples, families, and society. Knowing that sexual desire is not love, and that sexual activity motivated by craving always harms myself as well as others, I am determined not to engage in sexual relations without true love and a deep, long-term commitment made known to my family and friends. I will do everything in my power to protect children from sexual abuse and to prevent couples and families from being broken by sexual misconduct. Seeing that body and mind are one, I am committed to learning appropriate ways to take care of my sexual energy and cultivating loving kindness, compassion, joy, and inclusiveness – which are the four basic elements of true love – for my greater happiness and the greater happiness of others. Practicing true love, we know that we will continue beautifully into the future.

4. LOVING SPEECH AND DEEP LISTENING

Aware of the suffering caused by unmindful speech and the inability to listen to others, I am committed to cultivating loving speech and compassionate listening in order to relieve suffering and to promote reconciliation and peace in myself and among other people, ethnic and religious groups, and nations. Knowing that words can create happiness or suffering, I am committed to speaking truthfully using words that inspire confidence, joy, and hope. When anger is manifesting in me, I am determined not to speak. I will practice mindful breathing and walking in order to recognize and to look deeply into my anger. I know that the roots of anger can be found in my wrong perceptions and lack of understanding of the suffering in myself and in the other person. I will speak and listen in a way that can help myself and the other person to transform suffering and see the way out of difficult situations. I am determined not to spread news that I do not know to be certain and not to utter words that can cause division or discord. I will practice Right Diligence to nourish my capacity for understanding, love, joy, and inclusiveness, and gradually transform anger, violence, and fear that lie deep in my consciousness.

5. NOURISHMENT AND HEALING

Aware of the suffering caused by unmindful consumption, I am committed to cultivating good health, both physical and mental, for myself, my family, and my society by practicing mindful eating, drinking, and consuming. I will practice looking deeply into how I consume the Four Kinds of Nutriments, namely edible foods, sense impressions, volition, and consciousness. I am determined not to gamble, or to use alcohol, drugs, or any other products which contain toxins, such as certain websites, electronic games, TV programs, films, magazines, books, and conversations. I will practice coming back to the present moment to be in touch with the refreshing, healing, and nourishing elements in me and around me, not letting regrets and sorrow drag me back into the past nor letting anxieties, fear, or craving pull me out of the present moment. I am determined not to try to cover up loneliness, anxiety, or other suffering by losing myself in consumption. I will contemplate interbeing and consume in a way that preserves peace, joy, and well-being in my body and consciousness, and in the collective body and consciousness of my family, my society, and the Earth.

Autism Organizations and Resources

AUTISM ORGANIZATIONS

- Autism Association of Western Australia: autism.org.au
- Autistic Self Advocacy Network: autisticadvocacy.org
- Autism Society (USA): autism-society.org
- Integrated Autism Services (Wales): awtistiaethcymru.org / autismwales.org
- National Autistic Society (UK): autism.org.uk
- The Art of Autism: the-art-of-autism.com

AUTISM RESOURCES

- Autscape.org (an annual conference in the UK specifically *by and for* autistic people)
- Easy Online Asperger's AQ Quiz: AspergersTest.net
- Strengths and Abilities in Autism, Altogether Autism Taki-watanga: https://www.altogetherautism.org.nz/strengths-and-abilities-in-autism
- Thinking Person's Guide to Autism: thinkingautismguide.com

- Understanding Autism (free online course), The Open University (UK): www.open.ac.uk/choose/unison/develop/my-knowledge/understanding-autism

- Understanding The Spectrum (A Comic Strip): https://the-art-of-autism.com/understanding-the-spectrum-a-comic-strip-explanation

- Women and Girls – an online training module, National Autistic Society (UK): www.autism.org.uk/what-we-do/professional-development/training-and-conferences/online/women-and-girls

Buddhist Organizations and Resources

BUDDHIST ORGANIZATIONS

- Amaravati (England): amaravati.org

- Buddhist Society of Western Australia: bswa.org

- Foundation for the Preservation of the Mahayana Tradition: FPMT.org

- International Zen Association: izauk.org

- Kagyu Samye Ling (Scotland): samyeling.org

- Palpung (Wales): palpung.org.uk

- Plum Village: plumvillage.org

- The Order of Interbeing: orderofinterbeing.org

- Triratna Buddhist Order: thebuddhistcentre.com

- Western Chan Fellowship: westernchanfellowship.org

BUDDHIST RESOURCES

- Access to Insight (Theravada Buddhism): accesstoinsight.org

- BIPOC sangha online: dharma.org

- BIPOC Voices: weekly Sunday sangha: spiritrock.org

- Buddha Educational Foundation: budaedu.org/en

- Buddhism in a Nutshell (online course): fpmt.org/education

- Buddhist Meditation 101 (online course): fpmt.org/education

- 'Courageous Conversations About Race. No 1': www.youtube.com/watch?v=d-U6Fwa-fjs

- Forest Sangha books (for free download): forestsangha.org/teachings/books

- FPMT Centers: fpmt.org/centers

- Global Sangha Directory: mindfulnessbell.org

- Sutta Central (early Buddhist texts): suttacentral.net

- The Art of Mindful Living: plumvillage.org/mindfulness-practice

- The Heart Sutra: plumvillage.org/sutra/the-heart-sutra

- The Rainbow Sangha (Insight Meditation): gaiahouse.co.uk

- The Rainbow Sangha (Zen Mahayana): plumvillage.org

- The Young Buddhist Editorial: youngbuddhisteditorial.com

- Zen Meditation (instructional video): throssel.org.uk/videos

Glossary

BUDDHISM

Ananda One of the direct disciples of the Buddha.

Attachment Grasping at or attaching ourselves to people, experiences or objects that we mistakenly believe will bring us happiness.

Avalokiteshvara The Bodhisattva of infinite compassion and mercy.

Aversion Avoiding people, experiences or objects that cause us suffering, rather than turning towards them and transforming our suffering into happiness and wellbeing.

Bodhisattva One who vows to become enlightened to relieve the suffering of all sentient beings.

Body scan Starting at the top of the head, scanning our awareness down our bodies, one body part at a time, noticing where we are stressed and tense.

Buddha Approximately 2600 years ago Shakyamuni Buddha (Gautama Siddhartha) achieved enlightenment. He went on to teach the Dharma to his disciples for 45 years.

Buddhist One who has taken refuge in the Triple Jewel.

Community of Interbeing Monastic order founded by Thich Nhat Hanh in 1966 in France.

Comparing mind Thinking that we are not good enough and that others matter more.

Compassion The wish that others be free of suffering.

Dhamma See 'Dharma'.

Dharma (Theravada/Dhamma) The teachings of the Buddha.

Dukkha Suffering.

Enlightenment Liberation from Samsara by awakening to the realization that our true minds are empty, spacious and luminous.

Equanimity The ability to see everyone as equal, to take a balanced approach to our dealings with others and to tread a middle path through life.

Following the breath Focusing attention on the in-breath and then on the out-breath.

Four Noble Truths The basic teachings of the Buddha that teach us how to transform our suffering into happiness and wellbeing.

Guided meditation A meditation led by a teacher or taken from a script from a book.

Impermanence Change is inevitable and nothing ever stays the same. Attachment to the notion of permanence is a primary cause of suffering.

Insight dialogue An interpersonal meditation practice that consists of meditative awareness, the teachings of the Buddha and interpersonal relatedness.

Interdependence No one person or object exists independently of the other. The rain cannot exist without the cloud, the cloud cannot exist without the rain.

Karma Consequences of our actions that either produce suffering (negative karma) or happiness and wellbeing (positive karma).

Kinhin The walking meditation that is practised between long periods of Zen sitting meditation.

Loving kindness to ourselves and others is the antidote to negative thoughts, feelings and actions.

Mahayana The goal of Mahayana Buddhism is the achievement of enlightenment for the benefit of all sentient beings.

Mantra A short phrase or group of words that are repeated either out loud or in the mind in order to assist with meditation.

Meditating on the breath The focusing of awareness on the breath as we breathe in and out.

Meditation The observation of the mind, body and feelings by the mind.

Metta Loving kindness.

Metta Bhavana Loving-kindness meditation.

Mindfulness is remembering to come back to the present moment when distracted by thoughts and feelings about the past or future.

Mitra A spiritual friend.

Monkey mind Our minds let go of one thought only to grasp on to another, similar to a monkey swinging through the trees, producing constant activity in our minds.

Noble Eightfold Path The Buddha's path to wellbeing and happiness.

No-self Our 'everyday' mind needs a contemporary self in order to navigate our lives. With true mind, however (which is empty, spacious and luminous), there is no self.

Order of Interbeing A global community of monastics and lay people based in Plum Village, France, founded by Thich Nhat Hanh in 1966.

Oryoki A set of nested bowls and eating utensils.

Pali Canon The original teachings of the Buddha.

Plum Village The first monastic practice centre founded by Thich Nhat Hanh in the West. It publishes an online global directory of local practice communities.

Preceptor The primary responsibility of the preceptor within the Triratna Buddhist Order is overseeing the ordination of new members and welcoming them into the Order.

Precepts A guide for acting morally, for example the Five Mindfulness Trainings.

Puja A ceremony that involves chanting and offerings.

Rainbow Sangha Plum Village LGBTQ+ online practice group. (And the name often given to any sangha which is for LGBTQ+ people.)

Refuge A formal ceremony in which one takes refuge in the Triple Jewel. One may also take refuge informally as a personal act of faith.

Reincarnation The cycle of death and rebirth.

Right Speech Speaking without malice or harmful intention.

Right View Understanding that there are two realities – contemporary reality in which we live our everyday lives, and absolute reality which is characterized by emptiness.

Samsara The cycle of death and rebirth that maintains us all in an existence of suffering.

Sangha Traditionally, the Buddhist community of ordained monks and nuns as referred to in the Triple Jewel. A more recent, popular meaning is a lay community of spiritual friends, for which a lower case 's' is used.

Sangharakshita A British Buddhist teacher and writer who was the founder of the Triratna Buddhist Community, born Dennis Philip Edward Lingwood (1925–2018).

Single focus meditation Focusing on an object such as the breath, an image or a mantra.

Sitting meditation Undertaken whilst sitting on the floor in the lotus or cross-legged position, resting on a meditation stool or cushion or sitting on a straight-back chair.

Sutra A religious text.

Thay The Vietnamese word for 'teacher'. Thich Nhat Hanh is affectionately known by this name within the Plum Village tradition.

Theravada A school of Buddhism based on the original teachings of the Buddha as recorded in the Pali Canon, with a strong emphasis on monasticism and personal liberation.

Thich Nhat Hanh, 1926–2021, was a Vietnamese Buddhist monk, teacher, author, poet and peace activist.

Triple Jewel The Buddha, the Dharma and the Sangha.

Triratna A Sanskrit term meaning 'Three Jewels'. The Triratna Buddhist Order focuses on the importance of community and spiritual friendships.

Vajrayana A development of Mahayana Buddhism, Vajrayana (also known as Tantric Buddhism) is characterized by the use of mantras and the visualization of deities.

Walking meditation is walking step by step, at a slow pace, in rhythm with our breathing.

Zen A development of Mahayana Buddhism, Zen is about understanding the true nature of mind directly through the practice of silence and sitting meditation.

Zendo A hall, room or other place that people go to practise Zen.

AUTISM

ADHD Attention Deficit Hyperactivity Disorder.

Anxiety is what we feel when we are worried, tense or afraid – particularly about things that are about to happen, or which we think could happen in the future.

Asperger's syndrome is an older term for a form of autism that has now been subsumed into Autism Spectrum Disorder in DSM-5 but is still in use in the World Health Organization ICD-10.

Autism is a lifelong developmental condition which affects how people perceive and interact with the world.

Autism assessment A medical assessment which considers an individual's development across the lifespan to specific criteria such as social interaction skills and sensory sensitivity.

Autism Spectrum Disorder (ASD) According to the Diagnostic and Statistical Manual of Mental Disorders (DSM-5), ASD is a developmental disorder that affects communication and behaviour starting in early childhood.

Autist An alternative term some autistic people use to describe themselves.

Autistic burnout Intense physical, mental and emotional exhaustion that affects all areas of a person's life.

Autistic spectrum See 'Autism Spectrum Disorder (ASD)'.

Depression can simply mean being in low spirits. At its most severe, depression can make you feel worthless and down on yourself – leading to hopelessness, despair and suicide.

Executive functioning A psychological term that covers, for example, organizational, planning, time-management and decision-making skills.

Gendering of autism There are marked differences in the way that autism affects men and women.

Info-dumping happens when an autistic person gathers so much information, usually about their special interest, that it all comes pouring out in a monologue.

Masking Hiding autistic behaviour by 'pretending to be normal'.

Meltdown A loss of control due to sensory overload, which may result in anger, rage, abusive language, challenging behaviour and self-harm.

Neurodiversity encompasses a wide range of neurological differences, such as autism, ADHD, dyslexia and dyspraxia.

Neurotypical people have no diagnosed neurological developmental disorders or conditions.

Overwhelm Intense feelings or sensory overload (such as loud noise, background noise, lights and crowds) that result in the need to find a quiet space.

Reasonable adjustment The UK Equality Act 2010 requires reasonable adjustments to be made to any element of a job which places a disabled person at a substantial disadvantage.

Rumination is going over a thought or a problem repetitively without coming to a satisfactory outcome, leading to an increase in anxiety or a deepening of depression.

Self-testing Diagnostic questionnaires, usually online, that provide an indication of whether a person is autistic or not.

Social anxiety disorder is anxiety triggered by everyday situations where you have to talk to another person or take part in a group activity.

Special interests bring autistic people great joy, as well as being valuable means for learning and connection. However, they can acquire an intensity that starts to take over other aspects of life.

Spectrum condition A spectrum condition, such as autism, is one in which the effect on a person's psychological, social and linguistic ability varies over a range of possible outcomes.

Stimming is self-soothing behaviour that includes arm- or hand-flapping, finger-flicking, vocalizations and rocking.

True autistic self is embracing one's true identity as an autistic person – and behaving and speaking authentically despite the potential constraints of the neurotypical world.

Bibliography

AUTISM

Attwood, T. (2015) *The Complete Guide to Asperger's Syndrome*. London: Jessica Kingsley Publishers (first published 2008).

Autism Society (2020) 'Facts and statistics.' Accessed on 7/5/2022 at: www.autism-society.org/what-is/facts-and-statistics.

Autism Spectrum Australia (2018) 'Autism prevalence rate up by an estimated 40% to 1 in 70 people.' Accessed on 7/5/2022 at: www.autismspectrum.org.au/news/autism-prevalence-rate-up-by-an-estimated-40-to-1-in-70-people-11-07-2018.

Bogdashina, O. (2013) *Autism and Spirituality: Psyche, Self and Spirit in People on the Autism Spectrum*. London: Jessica Kingsley Publishers.

Clements, T. (2017) *The Autistic Buddha*. Lancaster: Your Stories Matter.

Grandin, T. (2020) *Different...Not Less: Inspiring Stories of Achievement and Successful Employment from Adults with Autism, Asperger's, and ADHD*. Arlington, TX: Future Horizons (first published 2012).

Heath, S. (2016) 'The Eighth Degree of Autism.' In P. Wylie, W. Lawson and L. Beardon (eds) *The Nine Degrees of Autism: A Developmental Model for the Alignment and Reconciliation of Hidden Neurological Conditions*. London: Routledge.

Isanon, A. (2001) *Spirituality and the Autism Spectrum: Of Falling Sparrows*. London: Jessica Kingsley Publishers.

Mitchell, C. (2008) *Asperger's Syndrome and Mindfulness: Taking Refuge in the Buddha*. London: Jessica Kingsley Publishers.

Mitchell, C. (2013) *Mindful Living with Asperger's Syndrome: Every-day Mindfulness Practices to Help You Tune in to the Present Moment.* London: Jessica Kingsley Publishers.

Rodman, K. E. (2003) *Asperger Syndrome and Adults... Is Anyone Listening? Essays and Poems by Spouses, Partners and Parents of Adults with Asperger Syndrome.* London: Jessica Kingsley Publishers.

The National Autistic Society (2022) 'What is autism?' Accessed on 7/5/2022 at: https://autism.org.uk/advice-and-guidance/what-is-autism.

Wylie, P. (2014) *Very Late Diagnosis of Asperger Syndrome (Autism Spectrum Disorder): How Seeking a Diagnosis in Adulthood Can Change Your Life.* London: Jessica Kingsley Publishers.

BUDDHISM

Access to Insight (ed.) (2013) 'Admirable friendship: *kalyanamittata.' Access to Insight (BCBS Edition).* Accessed on 14/4/2022 at: www.accesstoinsight.org/ptf/dhamma/sacca/sacca4/samma-ditthi/kalyanamittata.html.

Cornfield, J. (1996) *Living Dharma.* Boston, MA, and London: Shambhala Publications (first published 1977).

Dhammika, Ven. S. (2006) *Good Question, Good Answer.* Singapore: Buddha Mandala Society. Accessed on 13/4/2022 at: http://ftp.budaedu.org/ebooks/pdf/EN226.pdf.

Dorjee, Lama D. (2013) *Stillness, Insight, and Emptiness: Buddhist Meditation from the Ground Up.* Boston, MA: Snow Lion.

Hanh, T. N. (1998) *The Heart of the Buddha's Teaching: Transforming Suffering into Peace, Joy and Liberation.* London: Rider.

Hanh, T. N. (2013) *Breathe, You Are Alive!: The Sutra on the Full Awareness of Breathing.* Berkeley, CA: Parallax Press.

Hanh, T. N. (2014) *No Mud, No Lotus: The Art of Transforming Suffering.* Berkeley, CA: Parallax Press.

Hanh, T. N. (2021) *Chanting from the Heart.* Berkeley, CA: Parallax Press.

Jiyu-Kennett, Rev. Master (2016) *Serene Reflection Meditation.* Mt. Shasta, CA: Shasta Abbey Press.

Laity, Sister Annabel (2019) *True Virtue: The Journey of an English Buddhist Nun.* Berkeley, CA: Parallax Press.

Loundon, S. (ed.) (2001) *Blue Jean Buddha: Voices of Young Buddhists.* Boston, MA: Wisdom Publications.

McDonald, K. (1984) *How to Meditate: A Practical Guide.* London: Wisdom Publications.

Plum Village (2020) 'May The Day Be Well' chant. Accessed on 14/4/2022 at: https://plumvillage.org/library/chants/may-the-day-be-well.

Ricard, M. (2013) *On the Path to Enlightenment: Heart Advice from the Great Tibetan Masters.* Boston, MA: Shambhala Publications.

Salzberg, S. (2018) *Loving Kindness: The Revolutionary Art of Happiness.* Boston, MA: Shambhala Publications (first published 1995).

Suzuki, S. (1970) *Zen Mind, Beginner's Mind: Informal Talks on Zen Meditation and Practice.* New York: Weatherhill.

The Dalai Lama (2004) *An Introduction to Buddhism.* Boulder, CO: Shambhala Publications.

Tsering, G. T. (2005) *The Four Noble Truths: The Foundation of Buddhist Thought, Vol. 1.* Boston, MA: Wisdom Publications.

Welwood, J. (ed.) (1992) *Ordinary Magic: Everyday Life as Spiritual Path.* Boston, MA: Shambhala Publications.

Yetunde, P. A. and Giles, C. A. (2020) *Black and Buddhist: What Buddhism Can Teach Us About Race, Resilience, Transformation and Freedom.* Boulder, CO: Shambhala Publications.